DEFENSE, SECURITY AND STRATEGIES

UNMANNED AERIAL VEHICLE PROLIFERATION AND EXPORT CONTROLS

DEFENSE, SECURITY AND STRATEGIES

Additional books in this series can be found on Nova's website
under the Series tab.

Additional E-books in this series can be found on Nova's website
under the E-book tab.

DEFENSE, SECURITY AND STRATEGIES

UNMANNED AERIAL VEHICLE PROLIFERATION AND EXPORT CONTROLS

MAKSIM KORJUS

EDITOR

NOVINKA

New York

Library of Congress Cataloging-in-Publication Data

ISBN: 978-1-62808-228-9

Published by Nova Science Publishers, Inc. † New York

CONTENTS

PREFACE

Since 2005, the number of countries that acquired an unmanned aerial vehicle (UAV) system nearly doubled from about 40 to more than 75. In addition, countries of proliferation concern developed and fielded increasingly more sophisticated systems. Recent trends in new UAV capabilities, including armed and miniature UAVs, increased the number of military applications for this technology. A number of new civilian and commercial applications, such as law enforcement and environmental monitoring, are available for UAVs, but these applications are limited by regulatory restrictions on civilian airspace. The United States likely faces increasing risks as countries of concern and terrorist organizations seek to acquire UAV technology. Foreign countries' and terrorists' acquisition of UAVs could provide them with increased abilities to gather intelligence on and conduct attacks against U.S. interests. This book examines the global trends in the use of UAV technology; U.S. national security considerations concerning UAV proliferation; and the U.S. export control system.

Chapter 1 - The global use of UAVs has increased significantly over time, raising concerns about their proliferation. MTCR and Wassenaar are the multilateral regimes that address UAV proliferation. MTCR seeks to limit the proliferation of weapons of mass destruction delivery systems, while Wassenaar seeks to limit the spread of certain conventional weapons and sensitive technologies with both civilian and military uses.

This report is an unclassified version of a classified report issued in February 2012. GAO was asked to address (1) global trends in the use of UAV technology, (2) U.S. national security considerations concerning UAV proliferation, (3) multilateral and bilateral tools to control UAV proliferation, and (4) coordination of U.S. efforts to limit the spread of UAV technology. To conduct this review, GAO analyzed intelligence, licensing, and end-use monitoring data, and interviewed U.S. and foreign officials.

Chapter 2 - The 113th Congress may consider reforms of the U.S. export control system. The balance between national security and export competitiveness has made the subject of export controls controversial for decades. Through the Export Administration Act (EAA), the Arms Export Control Act (AECA), the International Emergency Economic Powers Act (IEEPA), and other authorities, the United States restricts the export of defense items or munitions; so-called "dual-use" goods and technology—items with both civilian and military applications; certain nuclear materials and technology; and items that would assist in the proliferation of nuclear, chemical, and biological weapons or the missile technology used to deliver them. U.S. export controls are also used to restrict exports to certain countries on which the United States imposes economic sanctions. At present, the EAA has expired and dual-use controls are maintained under IEEPA authorities.

The U.S. export control system is diffused among several different licensing and enforcement agencies. Exports of dual-use goods and technologies are licensed by the Department of Commerce, munitions are licensed by the Department of State, and restrictions on exports based on U.S. sanctions are administered by the U.S. Treasury. Enforcement of export controls is conducted by these agencies as well as by units of the Department of Homeland Security (DHS) and the Department of Justice (DOJ).

Aspects of the U.S. export control system have long been criticized by exporters, nonproliferation advocates, and other stakeholders as being too rigorous, insufficiently rigorous, cumbersome, obsolete, inefficient, or any combination of these descriptions. In August 2009, the Obama Administration launched a comprehensive review of the U.S. export control system. In April 2010, Defense Secretary Robert M. Gates proposed an outline of a new system based on four singularities:

- a single export control licensing agency for both dual-use and munitions exports,
- a unified control list,
- a single enforcement coordination agency, and
- a single integrated information technology (IT) system.

The rationalization of the two control lists has been the Administration's focus to date. Interim steps have also been taken to create a single IT system and to establish an export enforcement coordination center. No specific proposals have been made concerning the single licensing agency.

In contrast to the Administration's approach, legislation was introduced to reauthorize or rewrite the EAA in the 112th Congress. The Export Administration Renewal Act of 2011 (H.R. 2122, RosLehtinen) would have renewed the currently expired Export Administration Act through 2015, updated its penalty and enforcement provisions, and provided stricter foreign policy controls on countries designated as state sponsors of terrorism. A separate title would have amended the Arms Export Control Act to permit generic parts and components for defense articles to be controlled differently than sensitive defense articles on the U.S. Munitions List. By contrast, the Technology Security Act of 2011 (H.R. 2004, Berman) would have rewritten the dual-use export control statute by giving the President the authority to control exports for national security and foreign policy reasons and to create the mechanisms for doing so. Each bill would, if passed, have implications for the President's reform efforts. In addition, the National Defense Authorization Act for FY2013 (P.L. 112-239), signed by the President on January 2, 2013, contains a provision to repeal 1998 legislation that placed commercial communications satellites (CCS) under munitions export licensing jurisdiction and to permit the President to determine the export control jurisdiction of CCS.

In considering the future of the U.S. export control system, Congress may weigh the merits of a unified export control system—the end result of the President's proposal—or the continuation of the present bifurcated system by reauthorizing the present EAA or writing new legislation. In doing so, Congress may debate the record of the present dual-use system maintained by emergency authority, the aims and effectiveness of the present non-proliferation control regimes, the maintenance of the defense industrial base, and the delicate balance between the maintenance of economic competitiveness and the preservation of national security.

In: Unmanned Aerial Vehicle Proliferation … ISBN: 978-1-62808-228-9
Editor: Maksim Korjus

Chapter 1

NONPROLIFERATION: AGENCIES COULD IMPROVE INFORMATION SHARING AND END-USE MONITORING ON UNMANNED AERIAL VEHICLE EXPORTS*

United States Government Accountability Office

WHY GAO DID THIS STUDY

The global use of UAVs has increased significantly over time, raising concerns about their proliferation. MTCR and Wassenaar are the multilateral regimes that address UAV proliferation. MTCR seeks to limit the proliferation of weapons of mass destruction delivery systems, while Wassenaar seeks to limit the spread of certain conventional weapons and sensitive technologies with both civilian and military uses.

This report is an unclassified version of a classified report issued in February 2012. GAO was asked to address (1) global trends in the use of UAV technology, (2) U.S. national security considerations concerning UAV proliferation, (3) multilateral and bilateral tools to control UAV proliferation, and (4) coordination of U.S. efforts to limit the spread of UAV technology. To conduct this review, GAO analyzed intelligence, licensing, and end-use monitoring data, and interviewed U.S. and foreign officials.

---

* This is an edited, reformatted and augmented version of United States Government Accountability Office, Publication No. GAO-12-536, dated July 2012.

What GAO Recommends

GAO recommends that State improve its export licensing database to better identify authorized UAV exports, that relevant agencies improve mechanisms for sharing information relevant to the export licensing process, and that State and DOD harmonize their UAV end-use monitoring approaches. The agencies generally agreed with the recommendations.

What GAO Found

Since 2005, the number of countries that acquired an unmanned aerial vehicle (UAV) system nearly doubled from about 40 to more than 75. In addition, countries of proliferation concern developed and fielded increasingly more sophisticated systems. Recent trends in new UAV capabilities, including armed and miniature UAVs, increased the number of military applications for this technology. A number of new civilian and commercial applications, such as law enforcement and environmental monitoring, are available for UAVs, but these applications are limited by regulatory restrictions on civilian airspace.

The United States likely faces increasing risks as countries of concern and terrorist organizations seek to acquire UAV technology. Foreign countries' and terrorists' acquisition of UAVs could provide them with increased abilities to gather intelligence on and conduct attacks against U.S. interests. For instance, some foreign countries likely have already used UAVs to gather information on U.S. military activities overseas. Alternatively, the U.S. government has determined that selected transfers of UAV technology support its national security interests by providing allies with key capabilities and by helping retain a strong industrial base for UAV production. For instance, the United Kingdom and Italy have used UAVs purchased from the United States to collect data on Taliban activity in Afghanistan.

The United States has engaged in multilateral and bilateral diplomacy to address UAV proliferation concerns. The United States principally engaged the Missile Technology Control Regime (MTCR) to address multilateral UAV proliferation concerns. Since 2005, the United States proposed certain significant changes to address how MTCR controls UAVs, but members could not reach a consensus for these changes. Also, while the Wassenaar Arrangement (Wassenaar) controls the export of some key dual-use UAV components, it does not control other dual-use technologies that are commonly used in UAVs. The Department of State (State) has also used diplomatic cables to address the proliferation of UAV-related technologies bilaterally. State provided to GAO about 70 cables that it sent from January 2005 to September 2011 addressing UAV-related concerns to about 20 governments and the MTCR. Over 75 percent of these cables focused on efforts by a small number of countries of concern to obtain UAV technology.

U.S. agencies coordinate in several ways to control the spread of UAV technology, but could improve their UAV-related information sharing. For instance, an interagency group reviews many license applications to export UAV technology. However, there is not a formal mechanism to ensure that licensing agencies have relevant and timely intelligence information when making licensing decisions. Also, State's licensing database cannot provide aggregate data on military UAV exports State has authorized, which may impair the U.S. government's ability to oversee the release of sensitive UAV technology.

The Department of Defense (DOD) and State each conduct end-use monitoring of some UAV exports, but differences in the agencies' programs may result in similar types of items being subject to different levels of oversight.

ABBREVIATIONS

BIS	Bureau of Industry and Security
CBP	Customs and Border Protection
	Commerce Department of Commerce
CIA	Central Intelligence Agency
DCS	Direct Commercial Sales
DDTC	Department of State Directorate of Defense Trade Controls
DECA	Defense Export Control Agency
DHS	Department of Homeland Security
DOD	Department of Defense
DOJ	Department of Justice
DSCA	Defense Security Cooperation Agency
DSS	Defense Security Service
ECCN	Export Control Classification Number
FAA	Federal Aviation Administration
FBI	Federal Bureau of Investigation

FMS	Foreign Military Sales
ICE	Immigration and Customs Enforcement
MTCR	Missile Technology Control Regime
MTEC	Missile Technology Export Control Group
NASA	National Aeronautics and Space Administration
NASIC	National Air and Space Intelligence Center
NEECN	National Export Enforcement Coordination Network
State	Department of State
UCAV	unmanned combat aerial vehicle
	Wassenaar Wassenaar Arrangement
UAV	unmanned aerial vehicle

July 30, 2012
The Honorable John Tierney
Ranking Member
Subcommittee on National Security,
Homeland Defense, and Foreign Operations
Committee on Oversight and Government Reform
House of Representatives

Dear Mr. Tierney:

The use of unmanned aerial vehicles (UAVs) has increased significantly in recent years.[1] UAVs have demonstrated their effectiveness in recent conflicts, such as the wars in Iraq, Afghanistan, and Libya, where they have been used for intelligence, surveillance, and reconnaissance missions, as well as attack functions. UAVs are also increasingly being used for civilian purposes such as border security, environmental monitoring, and disaster relief. For example, the United States used UAVs to help the Japanese government survey the damage to the Fukushima nuclear power plant resulting from the March 2011 earthquake. The growing sophistication and availability of UAVs poses risks for U.S. interests. Consequently, the United States has sought to limit the spread of UAV technology through bilateral diplomacy and by working with like-minded supplier countries through multilateral regimes such as the Missile Technology Control Regime (MTCR) and the Wassenaar Arrangement (Wassenaar).[2] In addition, the United States and other countries control some UAV exports through national export control licensing and enforcement efforts.

In response to your request, we have updated our 2004 report on cruise missile and UAV proliferation, focusing solely on UAVs.[3] This report is a public version of the prior classified report that we provided to you in February 2012, which addressed since 2005, (1) trends in the development, acquisition, and application of UAV technology worldwide; (2) U.S. national security considerations associated with transfers of UAV technology; (3) the extent to which the United States has engaged in multilateral and bilateral diplomacy to address UAV proliferation concerns; and (4) the extent to which the U.S. government has coordinated its export control efforts to limit the spread of UAV technology. The Departments of Defense (DOD), State (State), and Homeland Security (DHS) deemed some of the information in the prior report as classified, which must be protected from public disclosure, as did the Federal Bureau of Investigation (FBI) and the Central Intelligence Agency (CIA). Therefore, this report omits sensitive information about efforts by countries of concern and terrorists to obtain and use sensitive UAV technology, as well as details about the U.S. proposals that the multilateral regimes did not adopt. This report also omits sensitive information about U.S. uses of bilateral diplomacy to address UAV proliferation concerns, U.S. efforts to coordinate and use certain sensitive information as part of the licensing process, and U.S. government efforts to coordinate the enforcement of export controls on UAVs. Furthermore, this report omits the full text of two of the three recommendations contained in the classified report, as well as State's, DOD's, and the Department of Commerce's (Commerce) written comments, as these contained sensitive information. This report is part of a larger body of work involving export controls.[4]

To address these objectives, we obtained fiscal years 2005 through 2010 export control licensing and end-use monitoring data from Commerce and State. We also obtained DOD fiscal years 2005 through 2010 Foreign Military Sales (FMS) program and end-use monitoring data. Based on our analysis of the data and interviews with agency officials, we determined that the data were sufficiently reliable for our use. We reviewed Commerce, State, and DOD documents, as well as intelligence and open source private sector reports on the proliferation of UAV technology. In Washington, D.C., we met with officials from Commerce, State, and DOD involved in the licensing and transfer process, and those officials knowledgeable about U.S. activities within the two multilateral regimes that the United States principally uses to address UAV proliferation concerns. We also met with officials from agencies responsible for enforcing export control laws and regulations, including Commerce, DHS, and the Department of Justice (DOJ), as well as with U.S.

government analysts knowledgeable about UAVs. In addition, we met with U.S. embassy and foreign government officials in three countries—Israel, Italy, and the United Kingdom. We selected these three countries based on analyses of DOD and State data and open source reporting showing that these countries either had extensive experience operating U.S.-made UAV systems or were a UAV producer.

We also met with leading UAV manufacturers and industry associations in the United States, Israel, Italy, and the United Kingdom. In addition, we examined applicable laws and directives. Appendix I provides a more detailed description of our scope, and methodology.

We conducted this performance audit from October 2010 to July 2012 in accordance with generally accepted government auditing standards. These standards require that we plan and perform the audit to obtain sufficient, appropriate evidence to provide a reasonable basis for our findings and conclusions based on our audit objectives. We believe that the evidence obtained provides a reasonable basis for our findings and conclusions based on our audit objectives.

BACKGROUND

Used only sparingly in past military operations, UAVs are now making national headlines as they are used in ways normally reserved for manned aircraft. UAVs come in a variety of sizes and configurations, ranging from as small as an insect to as large as a small commercial airliner. In our work, we focused on mini, tactical, and strategic UAVs.

According to available analysis, mini and tactical UAVs constituted the vast majority of the UAV systems in operation from 2005 to 2011, while strategic UAVs included some of the most versatile UAVs, typically capable of operating up to 30,000 to 45,000 feet in altitude with a maximum endurance of more than 20 hours. Figure 1 briefly describes these three types of UAVs.

Category	Mini	Tactical	Strategic
Altitude	Low	Low to medium	Medium to high
Endurance	Short (about an hour)	Medium (up to several hours)	Long (ranges from hours to days)
Range	Close-range	Limited to line-of-sight (approximately 300 kilometers or less) (about 186 miles)	Long range
Example	Raven 	Shadow 	Global Hawk 

Source: CIA (information); DOD (photos).

Figure 1. Three Major Categories of UAVs.

Multilateral Export Control Regimes That Address UAVs

The two principal multilateral regimes that address exports of UAVs are the MTCR and Wassenaar. MTCR, established in 1987, is a voluntary association of 34 countries that share the goal of limiting the spread of ballistic and cruise missiles and UAVs capable of delivering weapons of mass destruction. Wassenaar, established in 1996, is a voluntary association of 41 countries that share the goal of limiting the spread of certain conventional weapons and sensitive dual-use items having both civilian and military applications.[5] Both are consensus-based, requiring that all members must agree to any proposed changes in regime documents or activities. In both instances, members agree to restrict exports of sensitive technologies by placing them on commonly agreed to lists and incorporating these lists into their national export control laws and regulations. Members also conduct activities in support of the regimes, such as sharing information about denied license applications and conducting outreach to countries that are not members of the regimes.

Wassenaar has two control lists: a munitions list and a dual-use list. The MTCR members control a common list of items, which is contained in the MTCR Annex. The Annex covers complete missile systems, including rocket systems and UAVs, as well as a broad range of equipment, software, and technology.[6] The MTCR Annex consists of two categories of items: Category I and Category II. Under MTCR, complete UAV systems can be controlled as either a Category I or a Category II system, depending on their range and payload capacity.

- Category I UAVs are considered the most sensitive, and include strategic UAVs capable of delivering a payload of at least 500 kilograms (about 1,100 pounds) to a range of at least 300 kilometers (approximately 186 miles). MTCR member nations considering the export of these UAVs commit to apply a "strong presumption of denial" standard regardless of purpose, meaning that such transfers should occur only on rare occasions and only in instances that are well justified under the MTCR Guidelines.
- Category II UAVs are considered less sensitive, consisting primarily of UAVs that do not meet Category I criteria, but are capable of flying at least 300 kilometers. While these items require review through national export control systems, these items are not subject to the MTCR "strong presumption of denial," except for exports judged by the exporting country to be intended for use in delivering weapons of mass destruction.
- MTCR members have agreed to a "no undercut" policy for all MTCR-controlled items, meaning that MTCR members have agreed to consult with each other before considering exporting an item on the list that has been notified as denied by another member pursuant to the MTCR Guidelines.

Laws Governing Arms Exports and Sales of UAVs

Several U.S. laws authorize the sale or transfer of export controlled technologies from U.S. companies or the U.S. government to foreign countries, or in certain cases foreign entities. The Arms Export Control Act of 1976, as amended,[7] provides the President the authority to control the sale or transfer of defense articles and services. Under the Arms Export Control Act, State's Directorate of Defense Trade Controls (DDTC)[8] licenses direct commercial sale (DCS) exports of defense articles and services on the U.S. Munitions List,[9] while DOD's Defense Security Cooperation Agency (DSCA) administers the FMS program under the supervision and general direction of State.[10] In addition, the Arms Export Control Act, as amended, also requires end-use monitoring for the sale or export of defense articles and services, and delegates these responsibilities to the same agencies that administer the program. DDTC administers the Blue Lantern program to conduct end-use monitoring for defense articles exported under DCS, while DSCA administers the Golden Sentry program to monitor the end-use of defense articles transferred through FMS.

In addition, the Export Administration Act of 1979, as amended, 11 provides the President the authority to control the sale of dual-use technologies on the Commerce Control List, including certain dual-use components. Commerce's Bureau of Industry and Security (BIS) administers this license review process, with support from the Defense Technology Security Administration and other agencies.[12] BIS also administers Commerce's end-use monitoring program for technologies covered by the Commerce Control List.[13]

The U.S. export control enforcement system consists of multiple agencies. Within DHS, Immigration and Customs Enforcement (ICE) investigates suspected export control violations involving both U.S. Munitions List and Commerce Control List items. In addition, DHS' Customs and Border Protection (CBP) inspects selected exports to determine whether proper licenses were obtained prior to shipment and may interdict suspicious items being shipped. Within Commerce, BIS' Office of Export Enforcement has authority to investigate violations involving Commerce Control List items. Within DOJ, the FBI can take the lead in certain export control investigations involving counterintelligence and counterterrorism. DOJ prosecutes suspected export control violations. Investigations can result in criminal prosecutions; fines; and imprisonment or administrative penalties, such as export denial orders barring a party from exporting any U.S. items for a specific period of time. Figure 2 shows the principal agencies that have a role in the export control process. [14]

There are also U.S. government agencies that gather and analyze information on the proliferation of UAV systems and related technologies and produce UAV-related threat assessments and other UAV-related information. The Director of National Intelligence serves as the head of the intelligence community, establishing objectives and priorities for collection, analysis, production, and dissemination of national intelligence. Moreover, the Defense Security Service (DSS) provides threat assessments in support of its mission to oversee the protection of U.S. classified information and data in the hands of cleared DOD contractors.

The executive branch is currently considering reforms to the U.S. export control system in an Export Control Reform Initiative, including the creation of a single control list and a single information technology system. This initiative could affect export control licensing and enforcement efforts involving UAVs and related technologies and components.

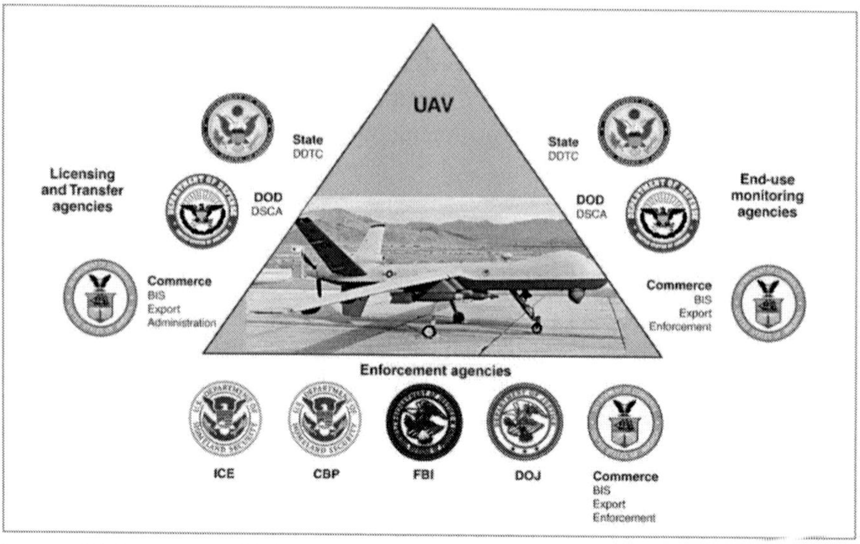

Source: GAO analysis of information provided by State, Commerce, DOD, DHS, and DOJ; Corel Draw (clip art).

Note: While DSCA does not actually issue licenses for military UAVs and related technology transferred through FMS, we include them since they manage the U.S. government's process for reviewing and making recommendations to State on transfers of such items through FMS. For the purposes of this report, transfers include defense articles and services authorized for sale through direct commercial sales, as well as defense articles and services that the U.S. government sells to foreign governments and international organizations through FMS.

Figure 2. Principal UAV Licensing, Transfer, End-Use Monitoring, and Enforcement Agencies.

Trends Show Rapid Growth in Global Acquisition, Development, and Military Application of UAVs

There has been rapid growth globally in UAV acquisition, development, and military applications. From 2005 to 2011, nations, including countries of proliferation concern and key allies, sought to improve their intelligence gathering and military aviation capabilities by developing and fielding their own UAV systems. Furthermore, militaries across the globe sought to expand the uses for UAVs, particularly in the area of armed strike missions. UAVs are also increasingly used in a number of civil and commercial applications, such as law enforcement, but national and international regulations place restrictions on most of these applications.[15]

Countries with UAVs Nearly Doubled in Seven Years

Our analysis of open source information shows a significant increase in the number of countries that acquired a UAV system since 2005. In 2004, we reported that approximately 41 countries had acquired a UAV.[16] Our review of current U.S. export licensing data and open source materials found that this number grew over the intervening period to at least 76 countries. Figure 3 provides a global picture of the countries that have acquired UAVs.

According to available analysis, the majority of foreign UAVs that countries have acquired fall within the tactical category. Tactical UAVs primarily conduct intelligence, surveillance, and reconnaissance missions and typically have a limited operational range of at most 300 kilometers. However, some more advanced varieties are capable of performing intelligence collection, targeting, or attack missions. Mini UAVs were also frequently acquired across the globe during this period.

Several countries acquired UAVs from the United States, which increased its export of this technology from fiscal year 2005 to December 2011. U.S. export licensing data show an upward trend in approved military and dual-use UAV export licenses since 2005. Approved dual-use export licenses totaled almost $4 million from fiscal year 2005 to fiscal year 2010. For military DCS licenses over this same period, the total value of approved UAV licenses was at least $240 million.[17] In addition, the United States sold $144 million worth of UAV technology to other governments through the FMS program from fiscal years 2005 to 2010. The United States exported a variety of UAV systems, ranging from mini UAVs, such as the Raven, to strategic systems, such as the Predator and Global Hawk. To date, the United States has exported a limited number of Category I UAV systems, sending Reapers and Predators to Italy, Reapers to the United Kingdom, and Global Hawk airframes to Germany and NATO as part of joint UAV development programs. Officials from two U.S. defense manufacturers that produce strategic UAVs both stated that there is additional demand internationally for Category I UAVs but that they are unable to meet this demand due to export control restrictions placed on these systems by the U.S. government.

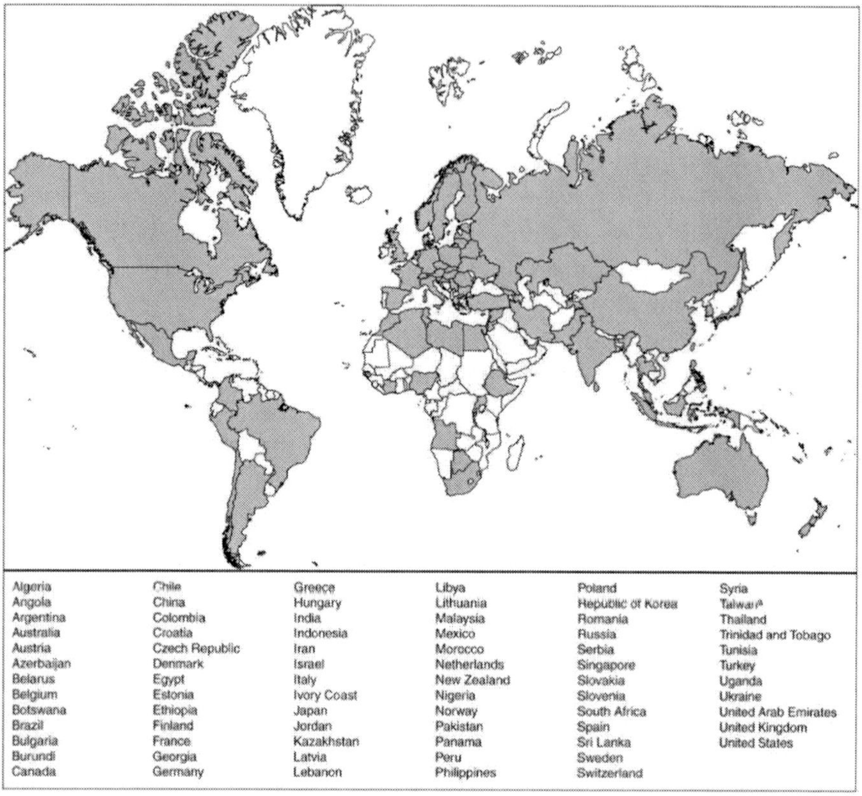

Source: GAO analysis of various unclassified sources; Map Resources (map).
Note: Shaded countries have acquired UAV systems.
[a] Although the United States does not have diplomatic relations with Taiwan, we have listed it as a separate country because whenever the laws of the United States refer or relate to foreign countries, nations, states, governments, or similar entities, such terms shall include and shall apply to Taiwan. For the purposes of this report, Taiwan is included as a country.

Figure 3. Map of Countries That Acquired UAVs by December 2011.

Many countries acquired their UAVs from Israel, one of the predominant global exporters of this technology, according to available analysis. Several key allies, such as Germany, France, and the United Kingdom, leased or purchased UAVs from Israel for use in Afghanistan. Countries such as India, Russia, and Georgia also acquired UAVs from Israel.

According to Israeli UAV manufacturers, exports are critical to their UAV programs as they account for the majority of revenue from the production of a system. Israel exports both mini and tactical UAVs. In addition, Israel has exported the Heron I, which is a strategic UAV. Company officials at an Israeli manufacturer told us they are currently marketing the Heron TP, a strategic UAV that would fall under Category I of the MTCR (see fig. 4). Because Israel has made several changes to its export control regime since 2006 and is one of the three countries that we visited, we provide further details about the changes that Israel has made to its export control regime since 2006 in appendix III.

Source: NASIC.

Figure 4. Heron TP-Strategic UAV Produced by an Israeli Manufacturer.

Countries acquired UAVs from a limited number of other exporters, including Austria, South Africa, and Italy, who used foreign sales to support their developing UAV industries. An Austrian company produces a tactical rotary UAV that has been exported to a range of countries such as the United

Arab Emirates and a South African company produces a range of systems for export including both mini and tactical UAVs. In addition, an Italian manufacturer has produced and exported the Falco UAV system to Pakistan.

Countries of Concern and U.S. Allies Developed and Fielded UAVs

Both countries of concern and U.S. allies sought to develop and field their own UAVs from 2005 to the present. We were informed that the number of countries developing UAVs has increased dramatically from 2005 to the present. Currently, there are over 50 countries developing more than 900 different UAV systems. This growth is attributed to countries seeing the success of the United States with UAVs in Iraq and Afghanistan and deciding to invest resources into UAV development to compete economically and militarily in this emerging area. We were also told that these programs benefited significantly from the availability of commercial UAV technology. Countries such as China and Iran made advances in UAV technology and successfully fielded a number of systems. China has pursued UAV development to obtain capabilities equal to current Western systems. Like many countries, China is developing mini and tactical UAV systems, but is also one of a small number of countries developing larger and more advanced systems, such as high-speed UAVs that are specially designed for combat.[18] Iran has developed and fielded tactical UAVs that are less sophisticated than Western designs, but still can perform missions, such as intelligence, surveillance, and reconnaissance and one-way strike missions.

Throughout this period, the United States and Israel were the world leaders in UAV development. Both countries developed and successfully fielded a wide range of mini and tactical UAVs and also produced MTCR Category I systems. Israel and the United States invested in the development of new varieties of systems, such as rotary-wing UAVs, unmanned cargo aircraft, and advanced handheld micro UAVs.

Many other nations have initiated their own UAV development programs. Countries such as South Africa, Singapore, Turkey, and nations in Western Europe, each developed UAVs alone or in cooperation with others. We were informed that many countries chose tactical UAVs for their development program. Tactical UAVs were chosen because they can easily incorporate available dual-use technology. Countries such as Italy, Germany, and South Africa have fielded and subsequently exported their UAV systems. In the last few years, countries such as Turkey, Russia, South Africa, and European consortiums established plans to develop their own strategic UAVs. According to available analysis, interest in armed UAVs has increased and development of these systems is expanding. However, in the near term, it is likely that only established UAV developers will be able to produce these systems, given the technical expertise required to successfully integrate weapons onto a UAV.

UAV Military Applications Increased, but Civilian and Commercial Applications Remain Limited

We were told that the variety of applications for UAVs and U.S. military use of them has grown since 2005, although the majority of UAVs have been used for military intelligence, surveillance, and reconnaissance missions. While U.S. UAVs primarily perform intelligence, surveillance, and reconnaissance missions, the United States has also armed many of its strategic UAVs, such as the Predator and the Reaper, and is in the process of arming tactical UAVs, such as the Shadow. DOD reports that the U.S. military has increased its use of UAVs significantly, growing from just over 10,000 UAV flight hours in 2005 to more than 550,000 in 2010. In addition, the United States transferred armed Reapers to the United Kingdom in 2006 for use as part of NATO efforts in Afghanistan. Other countries are also seeking to expand the range of missions for their UAVs by pursuing systems with armed capabilities, according to available analysis.

Militaries now also seek new ways to use this technology. For example, some military units use miniature handheld rotary UAVs, according to available analysis. The United States and other nations are researching specially designed high-speed unmanned combat aerial vehicles (UCAV) that can include stealth technology that will allow them to evade radar detection. The proposed design for the U.S. Navy UCAV currently in development is provided in figure 5. Additionally, the U.S. military recently began evaluating unmanned helicopter systems for use as cargo transport vehicles to free up pilots needed for critical combat missions.

UAV industry groups, manufacturers, and market analysts stated that civil and commercial UAV applications continue to grow, even though current national and international airspace regulations place restrictions on most of these activities. In 2008, we reported that there were potential civil uses for UAVs, such as law enforcement and disaster monitoring, as well as commercial applications, such as real estate photography and pipeline surveying.[19] Since then, civilian government entities—such as CBP, the National Aeronautics and Space Administration (NASA), the National Oceanic and Atmospheric Administration, and local law enforcement agencies—have acquired and used UAVs. NASA, for instance, used the Global Hawk system to track climate patterns in the arctic. Countries such as Australia, Brazil, and Japan used UAVs for purposes such as law enforcement, border protection, crop dusting, and environmental monitoring. These uses, however, are restricted by current national and international airspace regulations. In the United States, the Federal Aviation Administration (FAA) requires that a UAV operator obtain either a Special Airworthiness Certification or a Certificate of Authorization to fly a UAV.[20] From 2005 to 2011, FAA issued 88 Special Airworthiness Certificates and as of March 2011 had 264 active Certificates of Authorization. Other countries' restrictions can be even more limiting, according to FAA officials. Italian defense officials we spoke with stated that their regulations require a certification for each UAV and allow flights only in a specially designated off-shore corridor. In Israel, the military controls the country's airspace and does not permit the use of nonmilitary UAVs, according to U.S. embassy and Israeli officials.

Source: DOD.

Figure 5. Northrop Grumman's X-47B UCAV.

Governments recognize the interest in UAV civilian and commercial applications and are addressing this issue. In the United States, FAA is developing regulations to permit greater use of small UAVs inside some U.S. airspace and plans to draft and publish these regulations by 2013. Other countries also have taken steps to address this issue. For instance, officials from the United Kingdom's Civil Aviation Authority stated that they had established special airspace corridors for UAVs, which allow for testing and system development. Also, in October of 2011, Italian UAV companies announced that they had performed joint test flights of their systems within civilian airspace for the first time. The International Civil Aviation Organization, an organization that governs international airspace and assists with the establishment of common national airspace regulations, has a task force working to address obstacles to integrating UAVs in national and international airspace. Organizations such as the International Civil Aviation Organization and FAA have identified several issues, including establishing (1) signal frequencies and bandwidths for UAVs to use without disrupting other transmissions; (2) standards for "sense and avoid" technology to help UAVs avoid mid-air collisions; and (3) airworthiness certification standards that establish the required specifications for UAVs to be allowed to fly. Once these issues are addressed, UAV market analysts estimate that the civil and commercial markets for these systems have a strong potential for growth.

UAV Proliferation Presents Risks for the United States, but Selected Transfers Support Its Interests

The United States likely faces increasing risks as additional countries of concern and terrorist organizations acquire UAV technology. UAVs can provide countries and terrorists organizations with increased abilities to gather intelligence on and conduct attacks against U.S. interests. Alternatively, selected transfers of U.S. UAV technology support U.S. objectives by increasing allies' capabilities and by strengthening the industrial base for UAV production in the United States.

Foreign Countries' UAV Acquisition Puts U.S. Military Assets at Risk

Available analysis has determined that foreign countries' acquisition of UAVs can pose a threat because it puts U.S. military assets at increased risk of intelligence collection and attack. We were told that the significant growth in the number of countries that have acquired UAVs, including key countries of concern, has increased the threat to the United States. Because some types of UAVs are relatively inexpensive and have short development cycles, they offer even less wealthy countries a cost-effective way of obtaining new or improved military capabilities that can pose risks to the United States and its allies.

We were informed that currently, the potential threat to the United States primarily involves tactical UAVs, rather than more sophisticated, strategic systems. However, according to available analysis, countries of concern are pursuing more advanced UAVs through acquisitions from foreign suppliers and indigenous development. Such UAVs would be capable of flying higher, longer, and further and would be capable of a wider range of missions.

According to a publicly released DSS report, many countries of concern seek to illegally obtain U.S. UAV technology as part of their strategy to advance their UAV capabilities. DSS reported in 2009 that foreign targeting of U.S. UAV technology through both overt and covert collection efforts had increased dramatically in recent years.[21] According to DSS, the United States' acknowledged status as a global leader in UAV development makes the U.S. defense industry a primary focus of foreign collection attempts. The targeted technologies included engines, optics sensors, communications gear, and guidance and navigation systems.

We were informed that by acquiring UAVs, countries can enhance their capability to gather intelligence, surveillance, and reconnaissance information on U.S. forces and other assets. UAVs can allow countries to collect potentially harmful data on the location, strength, and movement of U.S. troops that can be used to more effectively plan or conduct attacks against U.S. interests. Available analysis also suggests that the use of UAVs by foreign parties to gather information on U.S. military activities has already taken place. We were informed that as more countries acquire UAVs, such intelligence, surveillance, and reconnaissance collection efforts are likely to increase.

Hostile countries could also use UAVs to attack U.S. interests. While only a limited number of countries have fielded lethal or weaponized UAVs, this threat is anticipated to grow, given the number of countries pursuing the acquisition or development of such systems, including countries of concern.[22] According to others' analysis, as the number of countries with such capabilities increases, it will likely alter the nature of future conflicts because countries will be able to field a larger number of strike assets without risking their manned aircraft.

Terrorist Organizations Could Use UAVs to Harm U.S. Interests, but Factors May Limit the Near-Term Risk

Available analysis has also shown that terrorist organizations' acquisition of UAVs to harm U.S. interests poses a risk for the United States. Certain terrorist organizations have acquired or are developing some form of UAV technology. For the most part, these organizations are currently limited to using smaller, more rudimentary UAVs, such as radio-controlled aircraft that are available worldwide from hobby shops or through the Internet. Hezbollah is one terrorist organization that has acquired and used UAV technology to date.

Although no terrorist organization has successfully carried out an attack with a UAV to date, available analysis has found that there are likely some terrorist organizations interested in using UAVs to deliver both conventional and unconventional weapons. For example, in September 2011, the FBI arrested an individual in the United States on charges that he planned to crash radio-controlled unmanned airplanes loaded with explosives into the U.S. Capitol and the Pentagon.

Available analysis has noted that there are likely advantages to using UAVs in terrorist attacks, but also factors that may limit the near-term risk. For instance, in certain situations, small UAVs could potentially be more precise in conducting terrorist attacks than using other items, such as mortars or rockets. The impact of such attacks might be lessened though, given the inability of small UAVs to carry large explosives. However, if terrorists were able to equip UAVs with even a small quantity of chemical or biological weapons an attack could potentially produce lethal results. Certain challenges were cited in acquiring the technology and expertise necessary to field a UAV sophisticated enough to carry out more destructive attacks with conventional weapons. Larger, more sophisticated systems would potentially also be harder to operate without detection.

Transfers of U.S. UAV Technology Increase Allies' Capabilities and Strengthen the Industrial Base for UAV Production

Although UAV proliferation poses risks, the U.S. government has determined that selected transfers of UAV technology can further national security objectives. The transfer of U.S. UAV systems to allies provides these countries with increased capabilities to contribute to U.S. efforts globally. It also helps ensure that allies' military equipment is interoperable with that of U.S. forces. Allies have used UAVs acquired from the United States to support a variety of U.S. objectives. For instance, coalition partners have successfully deployed U.S. UAVs to assist in the wars in Afghanistan and Iraq. The U.S. Air Force reported that Italy effectively used Predators purchased from the United States to locate roadside bombs and weapons caches in Iraq, supporting coalition efforts to stabilize the country in advance of national elections. Italy and the United Kingdom also successfully deployed U.S. UAVs in Afghanistan to collect intelligence, surveillance, and reconnaissance data on Taliban activity. State officials said that allowing such sales improved Italy's and the United Kingdom's abilities to function with the United States in an interoperable manner and provided U.S. and NATO commanders with additional assets. Allies also used UAVs purchased from the United States in support of such U.S. security objectives as counternarcotics and counterterrorism operations.

Additionally, DOD has noted the importance of allowing selected transfers of UAV technology in order to strengthen the U.S. industrial base for UAV production. According to some U.S. government officials, the ability to sell American UAVs to foreign purchasers helps defray the U.S. government's acquisition costs. U.S. government officials also noted that opening larger potential markets to American UAV producers provides additional incentives for producers to invest resources in the research and development of UAV systems, and helps the United States retain a technological lead over foreign UAV producers.

According to private sector representatives, UAVs are one of the most important growth sectors in the defense industry and provide significant opportunities for economic benefits if U.S. companies can remain competitive in the global UAV market.

The United States Has Used Diplomacy to Address UAV Proliferation Concerns with Limited Results

The United States has used multilateral and bilateral diplomacy to address UAV technology advances and proliferation concerns. For instance, to address advances in UAV technology, the United States proposed several changes to the MTCR; however, MTCR members agreed to only one change. Moreover, nonmembers continue to acquire, develop, and export UAV technology. In addition to multilateral diplomacy, the United States used bilateral diplomacy in the form of demarches to foreign governments to address specific UAV proliferation concerns with countries.[23]

The United States Made Proposals to Address the Proliferation of UAVs through the MTCR but Members Did Not Agree to Most of the Changes

The United States proposed changes to address how the MTCR applies to UAVs, but MTCR members only reached a consensus to accept one of the changes. The United States principally focused these efforts through the MTCR because it addresses the potential use of UAVs to deliver weapons of mass destruction, according to State. According to documents provided by State and State officials, the United States proposed six UAV-related changes to the MTCR Annex and members accepted one.

The five U.S.-sponsored UAV-related proposals that were not adopted were closely related. They were significant since they would have resulted in moving some UAVs currently categorized under MTCR Category I to Category II, according to State documents and State and DOD officials. However, MTCR members could not achieve a consensus to adopt the proposals. As we reported in 2004, both MTCR and Wassenaar use a consensus process that makes decision making difficult. MTCR last discussed these U.S. proposals in 2008 and removed them from its agenda the following year, pursuant to MTCR rules.

MTCR members have adopted a total of 22 UAV-related technical changes during the 2005 to 2011 period, according to State. For instance, MTCR members adopted controls on turboprop systems used in Category I UAVs and inertial navigation systems in Category II UAVs, according to State officials. However, according to available analysis, only 7 percent of UAV systems are subject to MTCR's strictest controls.

The United States Made Proposals to Address the Proliferation of UAVRelated Dual-Use Technologies, but Wassenaar Does Not Control Some Key Technologies

The United States proposed three major changes to the Wassenaar control list, which members adopted. The first, adopted in 2005, added to the control list equipment and components specially designed to convert manned aircraft to UAVs, as well as equipment specially designed to control UAVs and guidance and control systems for integration into UAVs, among other things. The second, adopted in 2007, added to the control list, engines designed or modified to power a UAV above 50,000 feet. The third, adopted in 2008, refined the control policy on navigation, altitude, and guidance and control systems for UAVs.

While Wassenaar applies to the export of some military and dual-use systems used on UAVs, it docs not apply to other dual-use enabling technologies, according to available analysis. Some of these dual-use technologies are critical to the development of UAV programs in certain countries of concern; however, they are difficult to control because they have other commercial applications.

Some Countries of UAV Proliferation Concern Are Not MTCR or Wassenaar Members

Regime members agree to provide greater scrutiny to trade in technologies identified as sensitive by the regimes through their national laws and regulations. Regime members also share license application denial and other information. Our most recent work shows that some countries that produce and export UAVs do not belong to MTCR or Wassenaar. This fact raises concerns about the potential for nonmembers to undermine the regimes' ability to limit UAV proliferation.

The United States Has Also Used Bilateral Demarches to Address UAV Proliferation Concerns

In addition to employing multilateral diplomacy to address UAV proliferation concerns, the United States employed bilateral diplomacy, chiefly in the form of demarches, to address specific concerns with foreign governments. State provided to us approximately 70 cables containing UAV-related demarches issued to 20 foreign governments and a multilateral regime during the period from January 2005 to September 2011. Over 75 percent of the cables provided responded to efforts by a small number of countries of concern to obtain controlled and uncontrolled technologies for use in their UAV programs.[24] While the regimes do not control the proliferation of all enabling technologies used by countries of concern to develop UAVs, the United States has issued demarches to foreign governments even for exports of certain uncontrolled technologies when these were clearly to be used for a military purpose. In addition, State cables show that several countries took actions in response to U.S. demarches.

U.S. Agencies Coordinate to Control the Spread of UAV Technology, but Could Strengthen Their Approval, Monitoring, and Enforcement Efforts

U.S. agencies coordinate in a variety of ways to control the spread of UAV technology, but could strengthen their processes for approving, monitoring, and enforcing export control requirements on UAVs. First, U.S. agencies have established procedures for coordinating the review and approval of UAV transfers, but limitations in information sharing hamper these efforts. Second, DOD, State, and Commerce each conduct end-use monitoring of some UAV technology, but differences in the agencies' programs may result in similar items being subject to different levels of oversight. Third, U.S. agencies have coordinated UAV-related prosecutions and other enforcement actions, but the nature of UAV technology and general issues with export control investigations present enforcement challenges.

Agencies Use an Interagency Process to Review and Approve UAV Transfers, but Limitations in Information Sharing Hamper This Process

Various U.S. government agencies, including Commerce, State, and DOD, play a role in the process to review and approve transfers of U.S. UAV technology to foreign purchasers. These agencies' decisions are guided by regulatory controls that have been established to govern the transfer of both military and dual-use UAV technology. Controls on military UAV systems and related technology are outlined in the U.S. Munitions List, while controls on dual-use UAV systems and related technology are listed in the Commerce Control List. The Commerce Control List contains three Export Control Classification Numbers (ECCNs) exclusively dealing with UAV systems and related items: 9A012, 9A120, and 9B010.[25] Additionally, we identified at least 29 other ECCNs that include controls on components or materials that can be used in UAVs. Unlike the Commerce Control List, the U.S. Munitions List does not include sections that outline controls for UAVs specifically.[26] Rather, controls for military UAV technology fall under several more general U.S. Munitions List categories. For instance, applicable controls for complete UAV systems are contained in Category VIII of the U.S. Munitions List, which deals with aircraft and associated equipment more broadly. According to State and Commerce officials, U.S. controls on UAVs are primarily based upon the MTCR and Wassenaar control lists. In addition, U.S. law establishes unilateral controls that limit the transfer of various items, including UAV technology, to particular countries. For instance, State noted that the U.S. trade embargos on countries such as Iran, North Korea, and Syria cover UAV technology, along with a wide array of other items. Additionally, the U.S. government has enacted laws that suspend the approval of any transfers of items on the U.S. Munitions List, including military UAV technology, to China.

While State and Commerce are responsible for reviewing and approving export licenses for military and dual-use UAV technology respectively, the U.S. government has established several mechanisms to coordinate these decisions with other relevant agencies.[27] For instance, State and Commerce, as the lead licensing agencies, "staff" out license applications to other relevant agencies, including DOD's Defense Technology Security Administration, for their review. State and Commerce officials noted that it is particularly important to provide licenses to DOD for review since DOD officials often have the technical expertise regarding particular items. Additionally, many UAV-related license applications are reviewed by the Missile Technology

Export Control Group (MTEC). The MTEC is an interagency body that is chaired by State's Bureau of International Security and Nonproliferation. It includes representatives from State's DDTC, DOD, Commerce, NASA, and the Department of Energy. During the weekly MTEC meetings, participants can make recommendations to approve or deny licenses or propose conditions to be placed on these licenses. According to State, the MTEC assesses whether license applications are consistent with U.S. laws and regulations, nonproliferation policy, and international commitments. For instance, in one case, the MTEC and the Missile Annex Review Committee[28] worked with a U.S. UAV producer to determine what modifications the company needed to make to one of its existing UAV systems to ensure that it was not inherently capable of delivering at least a 500 kilogram payload to a range of at least 300 kilometers. The resulting design ensured that the UAV was classified as an MTCR Category II system and thus not subject to the "strong presumption of denial," if the company sought to export the system.

State and DOD also coordinate decisions regarding the transfer of military UAV technology through the FMS program. For instance, DOD procedures in its Security Assistance Management Manual specify that DSCA or State may initiate coordination to approve or disapprove a transfer within 5 days of receiving the information copy of the Letter of Request, which is a formal request from a country to purchase an item through FMS. DSCA consults with State on these requests in order to determine if there are any immediate objections to the proposed sale within the U.S. government. Further, State must approve any arms transfer through FMS.

Limitations in License Database

The U.S. government has authorized the export of a range of UAV technology, but database limitations impair its ability to oversee the release of such technology. The U.S. government approved the export or transfer of a range of complete military and dual-use UAV systems, as well as key UAV components, from fiscal years 2005 through 2010, but it has no comprehensive view of the volume of UAV technology it authorized for export. Specifically, State's licensing database was not designed to produce complete data on the number, types, and value of UAV technology that State has licensed for export. Since State's database organizes items by U.S. Munitions List category and subcategory, and the list has no dedicated category or subcategory for UAV technology, State lacks an effective means of querying the database to identify UAV-related licenses. In July 2009, State issued a request that exporters list in the "purpose" field of their export license application if an item was a “UAV-related license,” covered under certain subcategories within Category VIII of the U.S. Munitions List. State issued this request to assist it in routing license applications to the appropriate internal unit for review, rather than to facilitate monitoring of the volume of UAV technology authorized for export, according to State officials.[29] Although State has issued the request to exporters, it does not have procedures to ensure that exporters comply with this request and the request does not apply to UAV-related licenses involving items not covered by Category VIII. In announcing the request, State noted its intention to automate this process, but had not done so as of February 2012.

In contrast, Commerce’s database does allow for identification of UAV-related items falling under the Commerce Control List’s three UAVspecific ECCNs. However, it has limitations in determining the extent to which certain UAV components have been authorized for export. The Commerce Control List contains at least 29 other ECCNs that control items that are used in UAVs, but can also be used for other purposes. For items controlled under these 29 ECCNs, Commerce’s database does not provide a means for easily determining which items authorized for export are to be used in UAVs and which are to be used for other purposes, such as in manned aircraft. DOD’s system for recording FMS cases is better able to provide a complete picture of UAV technology that has been transferred overseas via FMS.

These limitations in the U.S. government’s licensing data impair the ability of U.S. agencies and Congress to oversee the release of sensitive UAV technology. As a result, U.S. agencies may face additional challenges in working to effectively counter UAV proliferation. For instance, U.S. officials may lack complete information on relevant, past licensing decisions, when determining whether or not to grant an export license for a particular UAV item. Additionally, these data issues reduce U.S. agencies’ ability to conduct analysis of denied UAV-related license applications to determine if there are particular trends in questionable parties’ attempts to acquire UAV technology, according to U.S. government officials.

Despite these limitations, we analyzed State and Commerce licensing data, as well as FMS data, to estimate the extent to which the U.S. government authorized the export of UAV technology in fiscal years 2005 through 2010.[30] In total, the U.S. government approved FMS transfers of complete UAV systems in 15 cases over the period.[31] Additionally, we identified 1,278 UAV-related licenses that State processed over the period. Of these, State approved 90 percent, denied 3 percent, and returned to the applicant without action 7 percent.[32] We could not accurately determine the number of approved licenses that were for complete UAV systems, given limitations in State’s database, but the data indicate that State authorized the export of several complete UAV systems including the Desert Hawk, the ScanEagle, and the Raven. From fiscal years 2005 through 2010, we identified 134 licenses to export dual-use UAV technology that Commerce processed. It approved 74 percent of these applications, denied 2 percent and returned without action 24 percent. Of the 99 licenses that Commerce approved, we identified at least 55 that appeared to involve complete dual-use UAV systems based upon the descriptions in Commerce's data. In addition to complete UAV systems, the U.S. government authorized the export of an array of UAV components and subsystems. Table 1 shows a breakdown of the estimated number of UAV-related licenses for fiscal years 2005 through 2010.

Table 1. Estimates of State and Commerce UAV-Related Licenses, Fiscal Years 2005 through 2010

Agency	License applications total	Licenses approved	Licenses denied	Licenses returned without action
State	1,278	1,150	36	92
Commerce	134	99	3	32

Source: GAO analysis of State and Commerce data.

The U.S. government authorized the transfer of UAV systems to a variety of countries over fiscal years 2005 through 2010. For instance, it authorized the transfer of military UAVs to NATO allies such as Denmark, Italy, Lithuania, and the United Kingdom, as well as other countries such as Australia, Colombia, Israel, and Singapore.

Limitations in Information Sharing

In addition to the U.S. government's limited ability to determine the volume of authorized UAV exports, U.S. licensing agencies have limited information sharing mechanisms with the intelligence community. Both State and Commerce officials stated that the intelligence community does not have a formal process in place to directly provide them timely and relevant intelligence to assist in the licensing process. For instance, intelligence agencies may be consulted by the MTEC on occasion, but they are not routinely represented at weekly meetings. Some intelligence agencies participate in the interagency Missile Trade Analysis Group, which is a State-chaired interagency working group responsible for stopping specific shipments of missile and UAV proliferation concern worldwide.[33] Although the group is not directly involved in licensing issues, State officials noted that representatives from State's DDTC and Commerce's BIS attend the group's meetings to help ensure a strong working relationship with licensing agencies. Moreover, State officials stated that because both the MTEC and the Missile Trade Analysis Group are chaired by State's Bureau of International Security and Nonproliferation it helps ensure coordination and information-sharing on issues affecting both groups.

According to State and Commerce officials, certain intelligence agencies previously had a more formalized role in the licensing process, but chose to remove themselves from it in 2008. For instance, State officials stated that certain intelligence agencies had previously participated in the MTEC and helped validate the bona fides of foreign parties in license transactions. Additionally, Commerce officials reported one intelligence agency had previously hired contactors to screen foreign parties in Commerce export license applications against intelligence reporting. According to Commerce officials, this agency decided to end its formalized support for the licensing process due to budget cuts and other priorities. State officials said that, since 2008, State has struggled to get timely and relevant intelligence information to assist in licensing decisions. Additionally, Commerce officials stated that they did not believe they were getting access to all pertinent intelligence information as part of their license review process. Some DOD officials also expressed concern with the lack of official mechanisms for the intelligence and licensing agencies to coordinate and noted that some derogatory information available to them on parties listed on license applications may not be getting factored into licensing decisions.

According to U.S. government officials, the administration is currently discussing how the intelligence community can provide better support to the licensing agencies. Additionally, Commerce noted that it has received funding to establish its own intelligence center, known as the Strategic Intelligence Liaison Center, within BIS, to fill the gaps caused when the intelligence community stopped reviewing Commerce export licenses. The center will, among other things, check the names of parties in license applications against intelligence systems, as was previously done by the intelligence community. While the focus of the center will be on Commerce export licenses, Commerce officials stated that they are working with other relevant agencies to ensure that the information the center generates is available to them, as appropriate. Commerce stated that the center was established as of the end of 2011.

Three Agencies Conduct End-Use Monitoring of UAVs, but Procedures Are Different for Similar Items

State, Commerce, and DOD each conducts end-use monitoring on some UAV-related exports and transfers. Since our previous report on UAV proliferation, all three agencies have taken some steps to increase their end-use monitoring of UAVs and related items.

In 2004, the director of the Office of Enforcement Analysis within Commerce's BIS issued a memo to his staff that highlighted the need to focus greater attention on conducting end-use monitoring of UAV exports. The memo identified certain types of items that should have priority for end-use monitoring, given their utility in developing UAVs. Unlike Commerce, State issued no specific guidance on how to target its end-use monitoring of military UAV technology. Although State has not issued UAV-specific end-use monitoring guidance, State has identified UAVs as an example of a sensitive commodity that might trigger a Blue Lantern check, given the negative impact on national security if the item were to be diverted or illicitly retransferred.[34] State officials said that they consider a variety of factors when making a determination as to whether end-use checks on sensitive items, including UAV technology, are warranted. For instance, State may be more likely to do a Blue Lantern check if the end-user has no established history with controlled items, if the number of items ordered by the end-user is more than would reasonably be needed, if the shipment involves an illogical routing, or if the purchaser is paying in cash or at above market rates.

Shortly after our 2004 report, DOD took steps to strengthen its end-use monitoring of UAV technology transferred via FMS. In March 2004, DOD announced that MTCR Category I UAVs would be among those items subject to enhanced end-use monitoring under the Golden Sentry program.[35] For those items subject to enhanced end-use monitoring, DOD officials stationed in the host country are required to conduct inventories of transferred items following delivery and at regular intervals thereafter to verify that the items are accounted for and being used in accordance with the terms and conditions of the transfer. DOD can also require enhanced end-use monitoring on non-Category I UAVs, if the transfer is deemed to be of significant risk to warrant such a step. DOD officials reported that, as of February 2012, there had only been one instance where DOD required enhanced end-use monitoring for a non-Category I UAV.[36] Items not requiring enhanced end-use monitoring are subject to routine end-use monitoring under the Golden Sentry program. Routine end-use monitoring is conducted in conjunction with other required security-related duties. For example, U.S. officials might observe how a host country's military is using U.S. equipment when visiting a military installation on other business. Given the large volume of defense articles transferred through FMS, DSCA officials have instructed DOD personnel to concentrate routine end-use monitoring efforts on a "watch list" of specific categories of items. DOD has included UAVs among the items on the watch list. However, some DOD officials that we interviewed, as well as officials interviewed by other GAO teams in 2011, noted that there was not clear guidance on the activities that constitute routine end-use monitoring and how to document these efforts.[37]

The majority of end-use monitoring done for UAV-related items has had favorable results, but agencies found problems in some cases. From fiscal years 2005 through 2010, State identified 45 UAV-related Blue Lantern checks that it conducted and Commerce identified 201 UAVrelated end-use checks that it conducted.[38] Of the checks State identified as being UAV-related, 66 percent resulted in favorable findings, 16 percent in unfavorable findings, and another 18 percent were inconclusive.[39] Of the checks Commerce identified as being UAV-related, 58 percent were favorable, 6 percent were unfavorable, and the remaining 36 percent had limited or inconclusive results.[40] Of the checks that were unfavorable, some identified significant concerns related to unauthorized end-users or end-uses. For instance, State conducted a Blue Lantern check as part of a request to amend a license application to allow for the provision of additional services to one country in support of a U.S. UAV it had already purchased. State found that the country was basing and operating the UAV in a manner that violated the U.S. government's prohibition against using U.S. Munitions List items in internationally disputed territory. Thus, the check was deemed unfavorable.

Differences in Agencies' End-Use Monitoring Programs May Result in Different Levels of Oversight for Similar Items

All three agencies have conducted end-use monitoring on UAV technology, but differences in their respective end-use monitoring programs may result in similar types of items being subject to different levels of oversight. Further details of these differences in U.S. agencies' end-use monitoring programs for UAVs are addressed in the classified version of the report.

U.S. agencies may also have differing levels of access to facilities and equipment when conducting end-use monitoring, contributing to differences in the level of oversight of exported items. Although DOD requires that countries agree to permit inventories and physical inspections as a condition of FMS transfers, State sometimes lacks this type of agreement from countries for items exported through DCS. In fact, U.S. government officials noted that some bilateral agreements prohibit U.S. officials from directly conducting end-use monitoring on State-licensed items. Even when State does have such authority, it inconsistently visits end-users to verify compliance with license conditions, in at least some countries. For instance, we reported in November 2011 that State infrequently visited end-users in Persian Gulf countries when conducting Blue Lantern post-shipment checks on night vision devices.[41]

Agencies Coordinated Efforts to Enforce UAV Export Controls, but the Nature of UAV Technology Creates Enforcement Challenges

U.S. agencies coordinated their UAV enforcement actions through several mechanisms, including the National Export Enforcement Coordination Network, and the Exodus Command Center, but officials acknowledged limitations with each. We have previously reported on challenges in enforcing export control laws and regulations more generally. Among other things, we found enforcement agencies have had difficulty coordinating cases and agreeing on how to proceed on investigations.[42]

The National Export Enforcement Coordination Network (NEECN) was designed to be a hub for coordination on export control investigations. Among other things, NEECN assisted law enforcement agencies in apprising each other of investigative leads, disseminating investigative leads to law enforcement field offices, providing support to ongoing investigations, and identifying proliferation trends. As of November 2011, NEECN was replaced by the new Export Enforcement Coordination Center, as part of the administration's export control reform initiative. To help ensure greater coordination, the administration has required key agencies to partner in this effort in contrast with NEECN, which was a voluntary effort and at times suffered from a lack of agency participation, according to some law enforcement officials.[43]

Another key coordination mechanism is the ICE-led Exodus Command Center. Enforcement agencies, including ICE and CBP, submit license determination requests through the center to confirm with State or Commerce whether a particular item requires a license, and if so, whether the required license has been obtained. During fiscal years 2005 through 2010, law enforcement officials used the Exodus Command Center for license determination requests involving UAV-related technology; however, details of these requests are designated as sensitive but unclassified and are not reported here. Law enforcement officials noted that while the Exodus Command Center is a key tool, license determination requests can take a significant amount of time, thus impacting their ability to move forward on investigations or other enforcement actions. In March 2012, we issued a report that explores in more detail the challenges that law enforcement agencies face in investigating illicit transshipments, including license determination delays.[44]

U.S. agencies have worked together to take certain enforcement actions against violators of export control laws and regulations on UAV technology. Based on our analysis of DOJ reporting on export control enforcement prosecutions from October 2006 through June 2011, we identified at least seven prosecutions involving attempts to illegally export UAV-related technology. For instance, in 2009, a District of Columbia couple pleaded guilty to making false statements regarding the export of autopilots for mini UAVs to China.

According to U.S. enforcement officials, they encountered certain difficulties enforcing export laws and regulations on UAVs that are common across all export control investigations. For instance, of the 34 closed investigations that ICE identified for us as being UAV-related in fiscal years 2005 through 2010, none of the cases resulted in a criminal prosecution. In the majority of the 34 cases, the investigations were closed as a result of investigators losing touch with the suspects outside of the country. We previously reported that many suspects in export control violation cases are located outside of the country and foreign governments may not always choose to cooperate with U.S. law enforcement officials.[45]

Law enforcement officials also identified two issues that make UAV cases particularly difficult to pursue. DOJ officials noted that it can be difficult to prosecute a case involving an export control violation, particularly those involving dual-use technologies, because proving the violation took place typically involves showing that the commodity in question was specifically designed for use in a technology or application requiring an export control license. For instance, in the 2009 case discussed previously, DOJ ultimately prosecuted the District of Columbia couple for making false statements and not for illegally exporting the autopilots to China. DOJ did this because prosecutors could not prove that the autopilots were specially designed for use in military UAVs, despite evidence that this was their intended use, according to DOJ officials. As part of the administration's efforts to move items on the

U.S. Munitions List to the Commerce Control List, Commerce issued a proposed rule in the Federal Register in July 2011 defining what is meant by specially designed and requesting public comment on the proposed definition.[46] The comment period for this proposed rule closed on September 13, 2011. After reviewing the comments submitted and further review of the issue, Commerce issued another proposed rule further revising the definition of "specially designed" in the Federal Register in June 2012.[47] The comment period for this proposed rule will close on August 3, 2012. In addition, ICE, CBP, and Commerce officials noted that it is often difficult for law enforcement officials to determine whether violations are occurring because many law enforcement officials lack the technical skills to differentiate controlled UAV components from similar components used in model aircraft or ultralights, which are not subject to export control restrictions. Commerce officials also noted that the rapidly evolving nature of the technologies for use in UAVs could make it more difficult for law enforcement to readily identify these technologies in the future. According to ICE officials, to provide law enforcement officials with the technical skills to identify UAV-related technologies, ICE has provided UAV training to its agents in multiple locations throughout the country.[48] Commerce has also provided technical training to law enforcement officials; however, this training did not specifically focus on UAV technologies, according to Commerce officials.

CONCLUSION

Multiple factors highlight past and likely persistent limitations of U.S. efforts to control the proliferation of UAV technology through the export control process. First, the key trends in the acquisition, development, and applications of UAV technology globally show enormous growth in demand for military uses of UAVs, including for lethal applications, and an increasing ability of countries to acquire or develop their own systems. While only a few countries will have a near-term ability to develop and field the most sophisticated systems, many are expected to have sufficiently useful UAVs. These could threaten U.S. forces and interests. Second, the U.S. government recognizes the risks related to the proliferation of UAV technology, but faces difficulties setting controls on systems and components that countries of concern are interested in obtaining. Third, the U.S. government used multilateral and bilateral mechanisms to restrict the proliferation of UAV technology to a great extent, but as we reported in 2004, the nonbinding and consensual nature of multilateral export control regimes can challenge the U.S. government's ability to achieve its objectives in these forums.

While technological advances and the consensual nature of the multilateral export control regimes complicate the task of avoiding widespread proliferation to U.S. adversaries, the U.S. government can take steps to better coordinate its efforts to address national security considerations through its controls on the transfer and export of UAV technology. For instance, some agencies have routine and formal roles in reviewing licenses, but others have no formal mechanism to share significant information with each other. In fact, the role of some agencies with potentially important information to provide has diminished in recent years. Furthermore, U.S. government efforts to provide reasonable assurance that UAV exports and transfers are used as intended are marked by differing levels of protection through State and DOD end-use monitoring activities. As we previously reported on a similar situation involving night vision devices for Persian Gulf countries, major differences in the two agencies' monitoring programs need to be harmonized. Finally, certain information that would be useful to executive branch and congressional decision-making is unavailable because State's licensing database cannot readily identify all licenses authorizing military UAV exports. Thus the U.S. government cannot readily identify the full range of UAVs it has authorized for export to foreign countries.

RECOMMENDATIONS FOR EXECUTIVE ACTION

We are making three recommendations:[49]

- As part of the Administration's export control reform initiative, we recommend that the Secretary of State establish a mechanism in the licensing database to better enable the identification of licenses authorizing the export of UAVs and related components and technologies.
- We recommend that all U.S. agencies with information relevant to the export licensing process should seek to improve mechanisms for information sharing.
- To close gaps in the implementation of UAV end-use monitoring programs that may limit the ability of DOD and State to adequately safeguard defense articles upon their arrival and basing, we recommend that the Secretaries of State and Defense take steps to

harmonize their approaches to end-use monitoring. Such steps might include developing a plan for how and when each agency's end-use monitoring approaches would be harmonized.

AGENCY COMMENTS AND OUR EVALUATION

We provided a draft of our February 2012 classified report to State, DOD, Commerce, DHS, DOJ, and the CIA for their review and comment. State, DOD, Commerce, and DHS provided written comments. State's, DOD's, and Commerce's comments discussed classified information and cannot be publicly released; however, we have included an unclassified summary of their comments, as well as those of DHS. State, Commerce, and DOD also provided technical comments, as did the CIA, which we incorporated in the report as appropriate.

State agreed with our recommendation to establish a mechanism in the licensing database to better identify licenses authorizing the export of UAVs and related components and technologies. According to State, the U.S. Munitions List is being rewritten to redefine its controls on UAVs and better differentiate them from controls on other military aircraft. State noted that these changes to the U.S. Munitions List, along with the introduction of USXports as the U.S. government's export control licensing case management system, will provide an opportunity to improve database collection and facilitate the identification of UAV licenses.

State, DOD, and Commerce agreed with our recommendation to take additional steps to establish better interagency information sharing. According to State, the administration is currently trying to address such concerns as part of its export control reform initiative. Both DOD and Commerce noted that as part of the administration's export control reform initiative, a new unit, known as the Information Triage Unit, is being established to facilitate information sharing among various U.S. agencies. To begin implementing the functions of the Information Triage Unit, Commerce noted that it has established a Strategic Intelligence Liaison Center. DHS and Commerce noted the role of the Export Enforcement Coordination Center with respect to the exchange of export control-related information among certain U.S. agencies.

State and DOD also agreed with our recommendation to harmonize their approaches to the end-use monitoring of UAVs. State said that it has and will continue to make improvements in its end-use monitoring program. State also said that the report lacks some critical perspective on the number and scope of transfers involving the most sophisticated UAVs. We acknowledge that the United States has to date transferred only a limited number of more sophisticated UAVs, but this does not lessen the importance of ensuring that UAVs the United States transfers to foreign recipients are well protected. Additionally, we note U.S. government officials we met with anticipate that the number of such UAVs transferred will increase in the future. Thus, the importance of effective U.S. end-use monitoring of UAVs will likely continue to increase over time. DOD stated that it welcomes the opportunity to work with State on the end-use monitoring issues raised in our recommendation.

Thomas Melito
Director,
International Affairs and Trade

Appendix I: Scope and Methodology

To assess the global trends in the development, acquisition, and application of unmanned aerial vehicle (UAV) technology worldwide since 2005, we obtained, analyzed, and corroborated private sector open source and U.S. government reporting on U.S. and foreign UAV activities from various sources and spoke to representatives of U.S. private sector associations representing companies that manufacture UAVs. For this report, we defined the term "acquisition" to mean those countries that have obtained complete UAV systems, as well as the countries from which they acquired these UAVs. We defined the term "development" to mean those countries producing and supplying UAVs and the systems they are building. The term "applications" addressed the tasks that UAVs perform and the limitations in their capacity to achieve these tasks. Private sector associations we met with included the Association for Unmanned Vehicle Systems International and the Aerospace Industries Association. We also interviewed representatives of UAV manufacturers in the United States, as well as various analysts within the U.S. government who track UAV issues. We also obtained copies of their briefs as well as some of their reports. In addition, to get a better understanding of the regulatory and technological limitations that affect UAV development, we met with officials from the Federal Aviation Administration. As our trend assessment dealt with global trends, we also met with industry, trade association, and foreign government officials in three countries—Israel, Italy, and the United Kingdom—and obtained reports on their UAV programs. We selected these countries based on analyses of open source reporting and Department of Defense (DOD) and Department of State (State) data showing that these countries either have extensive experience operating U.S.-made UAV systems or are important producers of UAVs and related components. We traveled to Patuxent Naval Air Station in Patuxent, Maryland, to gain a firsthand understanding of the current state of UAV technology, observing the U.S. Navy's Broad Area Maritime Surveillance-Demonstrator system and the Shadow 200. The Broad Area Maritime Surveillance-Demonstrator UAV is based on the Global Hawk platform—a strategic UAV—while the Shadow 200 is a tactical UAV in use by the U.S. Army that is currently undergoing modification for use by the U.S. Marine Corps.

To assess the national security considerations associated with the proliferation of UAV technology, we met with private sector and U.S. government analysts knowledgeable about UAVs. We also obtained and analyzed a range of private sector and unclassified and classified reports and briefings by the intelligence community discussing the threats associated with the spread of UAV technology to countries of concern and terrorist organizations. Additionally, we interviewed officials from State, the Department of Commerce (Commerce), and DOD to gather information on the key risks and benefits associated with the spread of UAV technology. To better understand the security considerations associated with transfers of U.S. UAV technology to U.S. allies, we met with foreign government and U.S. embassy officials in Italy to document the Italian Ministry of Defense's experience purchasing and operating U.S.-made systems. While in London, we were unable to meet with United Kingdom military officials knowledgeable about their experience purchasing and operating U.S. systems, but we obtained written responses to questions from the United Kingdom's Ministry of Defense and met with U.S. embassy officials familiar with the United Kingdom's experience.

To assess the extent to which the U.S. government used the multilateral regimes and bilateral demarches to foreign countries to address UAV technology proliferation, we obtained and analyzed classified State reporting cables documenting the results of the 2005 through 2009 Missile Technology Control Regime (MTCR) plenaries and other meetings. We also reviewed various MTCR and Wassenaar Arrangement (Wassenaar) documents, including the two regime's control lists and the various U.S. proposals submitted to the MTCR and Wassenaar. Additionally, we interviewed State, Commerce, and DOD officials to gather information on the steps that the U.S. government has taken through the regimes to work with other participants to control UAV proliferation. We also met with officials of the Wassenaar Arrangement Secretariat. We attempted to meet with MTCR officials, but were not able to due to scheduling limitations. To better understand the limitations of the multilateral regimes, we met with officials from State, Commerce, DOD, and other agencies. To assess the extent to which the United States used bilateral diplomacy to address UAV proliferation concerns, we obtained and analyzed approximately 70 demarches presented to foreign countries during the January 2005 to September 2011 timeframe that State provided to us.[1] We also interviewed State officials knowledgeable about the demarches. We did not conduct an independent assessment to determine whether our sample contained all the UAV-related demarches that State presented to foreign countries during this timeframe.

To assess the extent to which the U.S. government has coordinated its export control efforts to limit the spread of UAV technology, we obtained and analyzed fiscal years 2005 through 2010 export licensing and end-use monitoring data from Commerce and State. We also obtained DOD fiscal years 2005 through 2010 Foreign Military Sales program and end-use monitoring data. To assess the reliability of these various data sets, we conducted interviews with relevant agency officials, reviewed agency documentation, reviewed past GAO assessments of the databases used to produce this data, and conducted our own reviews of the data provided by the agencies. We determined that the data were sufficiently reliable for our use; however, we identified certain limitations, including with State's licensing database in particular, which are discussed further below. We also reviewed Commerce, State, and DOD documents and reports and met with officials in Washington, D.C., involved in licensing, transfer, and end-use monitoring activities from these three agencies. We also met with agency officials from Commerce, Immigration and Customs Enforcement, Customs and Border Protection, the Federal Bureau of Investigation, and the Department of Justice responsible for enforcing export control laws and regulations.

To analyze Commerce's UAV-related export control licensing data, we identified the 3 principal export control classification numbers (ECCNs) that exclusively control UAV systems and technology, as well as 29 additional ECCNs that include technology that could be used in UAVs, but can also be used for other purposes. To identify these ECCNs, we first conducted a search of the Commerce Control List to determine which ECCNs contained the terms: "unmanned aerial vehicle," "UAV," "unmanned aerial system," and "UAS." We also reviewed Commerce documentation discussing UAV-related ECCNs. Finally, we validated the choice of these ECCNs with officials from

Commerce and the Defense Technology Security Administration and made modifications to our list based upon their input. We validated our list of ECCNs with Commerce and the Defense Technology Security Administration because Commerce manages the database used to track dual-use license applications and the Defense Technology Security Administration is the main agency that Commerce uses for technical assistance in conducting license reviews. We then analyzed Commerce export licensing data and quantified the number of license applications associated with each of these ECCNs during fiscal years 2005 through 2010. However, in the final report, we chose to limit our discussion to only those licenses involving the three ECCNS that are UAV-specific. We chose to do so because, through our own analysis and interviews with Commerce and Defense Technology Security Administration officials, we determined there was not a reliable way of identifying which of the more than 7,000 license applications involving the other 29 ECCNs included items that were to be used in UAVs, versus those licenses that included items to be used for other purposes, such as in manned aircraft. Because our final analysis does not include any license applications involving these 29 ECCNs, our results may not have captured some UAV-related licenses; however, we believe the results are sufficiently reliable to provide a reasonable estimate of the number of UAV-related licenses submitted to Commerce in fiscal years 2005 through 2010.

State's licensing database is organized according to U.S. Munitions List category and subcategory and there is no specific category or subcategory for UAVs and related technology. Thus, to analyze State's UAV-related licensing data, we obtained data for more than 7,000 license applications that State had submitted to the Missile Technology Export Control Group (MTEC) during fiscal years 2005 through 2010. While the majority of UAV licenses go before the MTEC, certain UAV-related licenses may not be captured within the data State provided, according to State officials. For instance, certain sensors or other types of payloads used in UAVs, but also used in other types of aircraft, might not be reviewed by the MTEC because they are not considered missile technology controlled by the MTCR, according to State officials. Additionally, the data provided by State included a significant number of licenses that were not UAV-related and instead pertained to other types of missile technology. To better identify the UAV-related licenses, we identified 34 key terms to use in filtering the data. These terms included both general terms that are commonly used to describe UAVs, such as "unmanned aerial system" and "UAS," and also specific terms that are the names of key UAV systems that are produced in the United States and abroad, such as "Predator" and "ScanEagle." We validated these terms with State and the Defense Technology Security Administration. We validated the choice of these terms with State and the Defense Technology Security Administration because State manages the database used to track U.S. Munitions List-related license applications and the Defense Technology Security Administration is the main agency that State uses for technical assistance in conducting license reviews. We used these terms to assist in separating out those licenses that were UAV-related from those that were not. Nonetheless, we found that Direct Commercial Sales (DCS) data could not identify with certainty all licenses authorizing UAVs and related components without a manual review of tens of thousands of licenses. As a consequence, we could not accurately report the magnitude of DCS arms transfer authorizations for UAVs; however, we believe the results are sufficiently reliable to provide a general estimate of the number of UAV-related licenses submitted to State in fiscal years 2005 through 2010.

To analyze State and Commerce end-use monitoring of UAV-related exports, we obtained end-use monitoring data from both agencies identifying the number, location, and type of UAV-related end-use monitoring checks conducted in fiscal years 2005 through 2010. Both State's and Commerce's end-use data have limitations because the agencies' databases are not designed to provide a means of automatically identifying end-use checks that are UAV-related. As a result, both agencies developed queries using terms such as "UAV" and "unmanned aerial vehicle." Based upon our discussions with agency officials, we believe that these queries identified the majority of relevant end-use check records, but some UAV-related checks may not have been captured in the queries. However, we determined that the agencies' end-use monitoring data is sufficiently reliable to provide a reasonable estimate of the number and types of checks performed by the two agencies.

To analyze DOD's transfers of UAV technology via the Foreign Military Sales (FMS) program, we obtained from the Defense Security Cooperation Agency (DSCA) a breakdown of the number, country, and type of UAV technology transferred during fiscal years 2005 through 2010. To produce this data, DSCA developed a query of its 1200 system to identify relevant FMS transfers involving UAV technology. We also obtained Golden Sentry UAV-related end-use monitoring data from DSCA for the same period.

To ensure the accuracy of the information contained in appendix III, we provided a copy of this appendix to Israeli government officials, who provided technical comments. We have incorporated their comments as appropriate.

DOD, State, the Department of Homeland Security, the Federal Bureau of Investigation, and the Central Intelligence Agency deemed some of the information in our February 2012 report as classified, which must be protected from public disclosure. Therefore, this report omits sensitive information about efforts by countries of concern and terrorists to obtain and use sensitive UAV technology, as well as details about the U.S. proposals that the multilateral regimes did not adopt. This report also omits sensitive information about U.S. uses of bilateral diplomacy to address UAV proliferation concerns, U.S. efforts to coordinate and use certain sensitive information as part of the licensing process, and U.S. government efforts to coordinate the enforcement of export controls on UAVs.

We conducted this performance audit from October 2010 to July 2012 in accordance with generally accepted auditing standards. These standards require that we plan and perform the audit to obtain sufficient, appropriate evidence to provide a reasonable basis for our findings and conclusions based on our audit objectives. We believe that the evidence obtained provides a reasonable basis for our findings and conclusions based on our audit objectives.

APPENDIX II: LIST OF MTCR AND WASSENAAR MEMBERS

Table 2. List of MTCR and Wassenaar Members

MTCR	Wassenaar
Argentina	Argentina
Australia	Australia
Austria	Austria
Belgium	Belgium
Brazil[a]	Bulgaria
Bulgaria	Canada
Canada	Croatia[b]
Czech Republic	Czech Republic
Denmark	Denmark
Finland	Estonia[b]
France	Finland
Germany	France
Greece	Germany
Hungary	Greece
Iceland	Hungary
Ireland	Ireland

Table 2. (Continued)

MTCR	Wassenaar
Italy	Italy
Japan	Japan
Luxembourg	Latvia[b]
Netherlands	Lithuania[b]
New Zealand	Luxembourg
Norway	Malta
Poland	Mexico[b]
Portugal	Netherlands
Republic of Korea	New Zealand
Russia	Norway
South Africa	Poland
Spain	Portugal
Sweden	Republic of Korea
Switzerland	Romania[b]
Turkey	Russia
Ukraine	Slovakia[b]
United Kingdom	Slovenia[b]
United States	South Africa
	Spain
	Sweden
	Switzerland
	Turkey
	Ukraine
	United Kingdom
	United States

Source: MTCR and Wassenaar.

[a] Brazil is a member of MTCR, but not Wassenaar.

[b] Croatia, Estonia, Latvia, Lithuania, Mexico, Romania, Slovakia, and Slovenia are members of Wassenaar, but not MTCR.

APPENDIX III: ISRAEL'S EXPORT CONTROL SYSTEM SINCE 2006

According to Israeli officials we spoke with, the changes that have occurred in Israel's export control system since 2006 were significant because they elevated the importance of export controls. For this reason, this appendix provides additional information about these changes. According to Israeli officials we spoke with, in general, the changes are designed to encourage more interagency coordination and to facilitate enhanced enforcement of export control laws.

In July 2006, Israel established a single export control agency within the Ministry of Defense, named the Defense Export Control Agency (DECA). DECA is responsible for reviewing and consequently approving or denying applications for licenses that involve items, technologies, know-how, and services which are considered under the definition of defense exports.

According to Israeli officials and documents, in cases where a license application involves purely military items or dual-use items that are destined for a military end-user, DECA bears full responsibility, although it is required to consult with the Ministry of Foreign Affairs. In these instances, the licensing process is a two-stage process with a marketing license preceding the export license. In cases of applications involving dual-use items destined for a civilian end-user, the Israeli Ministry of Industry, Trade, and Labor bears the responsibility, while consulting with DECA. In these cases, the licensing mechanism is a one-stage process, as it includes the issuance and granting of the export license alone.

According to Israeli officials and documents, for license applications in which DECA bears full responsibility, a mechanism was established within the Ministry of Defense to coordinate the review of these licenses. This includes the establishment of advisory committees. In addition, a technical committee called the "MTCR Committee" reviews license applications involving possible technologies controlled by MTCR. That committee's task is to determine whether an item is contained within an MTCR control list and if so, what category.

According to Israeli officials and documents, by law, DECA is solely responsible for enforcing export control directives and regulations. Within the framework of that responsibility, DECA is often assisted by Israeli Customs, which in practice, enforces most of the directives and regulations. In addition, DECA is responsible for conducting outreach to companies that export military and dual-use items, technologies, know-how, or services.

According to Israeli officials that we spoke with, Israel also adopted export control legislation to control the export of both military and dual-use items, technologies, know-how, and services. According to Israeli documents, in July 2007, the Israeli Parliament enacted a new Defense Export Control Law, which entered into force in December of that year. This law elevated the importance of export controls in several ways, according to Israeli officials. For instance, Israeli officials stated that the law established a requirement for

Israeli exporters to register before applying for any export control license and to create a new position within the company—director of export control. According to Israeli officials, the law also established periodic reporting, record-keeping, and inspection requirements; provided for new administrative penalties such as fines, suspensions, and revocations of licenses; and strengthened criminal penalties for those found violating the law. Moreover, according to Israeli documents, the Defense Export Control Law led the Ministry of Defense to establish separate lists of controlled technologies—one based on the MTCR Annex, two based on the Wassenaar munitions and dual-use lists, and a third dual-use list for transfers to the Palestinian Authority.

The lists of controlled technologies are updated annually in two ways, according to Israeli officials. First, DECA meets with MTCR and Wassenaar Arrangement officials in outreach sessions conducted by the two regimes. The outreach sessions are designed in part to inform key countries that are not MTCR or Wassenaar Arrangement members about control list changes agreed to by member countries, according to Wassenaar Arrangement officials. In addition, DECA meets with export control counterparts from the United States, United Kingdom, Germany, and other countries, according to Israeli officials.

With respect to license application approvals, the Israeli government typically imposes certain conditions, according to Israeli government and industry officials. For instance, DECA requires manufacturers to obtain re-export approval for all controlled components not made in Israel from the country of origin as a pre-condition for considering a license application. In addition, DECA typically imposes certain license conditions, for instance, requiring end-users to sign an end-use or end-user certificate. According to Israeli government officials, approved licenses often state that technology cannot be transferred to a third party without authorization from DECA.

According to Israeli government officials and documents, with respect to license applications involving UAV technology, the Israeli government typically imposes additional licensing conditions as well. For instance, license applications must specify under which MTCR category the UAV falls, if any. According to Israeli government and industry officials, for MTCR Category I UAVs such as the Heron TP, the Israeli government has adopted a "presumption of denial" standard. In instances where authorization is eventually given to export a Category I UAV, it is limited to MTCR member countries only. In cases where authorization is granted to export an MTCR Category II UAV, these may be marketed or sold to MTCR nonmember countries only as long as they provide a declaration that they fully adhere to MTCR controls.

End Notes

[1] While the term UAV has been in use for some time, the Department of Defense and the Federal Aviation Administration, among other U.S. and international organizations, now use the term unmanned aircraft systems, or UAS, when referring to these systems. For this report, we use the term UAV because it remains the official term used by both U.S. and multilateral export control bodies.

[2] Multilateral export control regimes are voluntary, nonbinding arrangements among like-minded supplier countries that aim to restrict trade in sensitive technologies to peaceful purposes. Multilateral export control regimes are referred to as either regimes or arrangements, and countries invited to participate in them are variously referred to as members, participants, participating states, or partners. In this report, we use the term regimes and refer to participating countries as members.

[3] GAO, *Nonproliferation: Improvements Needed to Better Control Technology Exports for Cruise Missiles and Unmanned Aerial Vehicles,* GAO-04-175 (Washington, D.C.: Jan. 23, 2004). In GAO-04-175, we found that cruise missiles and UAVs posed a growing threat to U.S. national security interests; multilateral export control regimes and national export controls were limited in their capacity to address cruise missile and UAV proliferation concerns' and the U.S. government had performed little end-use monitoring to verify that exporters and foreign recipients complied with licensing conditions.

[4] For example, GAO, *Persian Gulf: Implementation Gaps Limit the Effectiveness of End-Use Monitoring and Human Rights Vetting for U.S. Military Equipment,* GAO-12-89 (Washington, D.C.: Nov. 17, 2011), and GAO, *Export Controls: Agency Actions and Proposed Reform Initiatives May Address Previously Identified Weaknesses, but Challenges Remain,* GAO-11-135R (Washington, D.C.: Nov. 17, 2010).

[5] Appendix II contains a list of the MTCR and Wassenaar members.

[6] The Annex is formally known as the Equipment, Software, and Technology Annex. The MTCR's documents include the MTCR Guidelines and Annex. The Guidelines define the purpose of MTCR and provide the overall structure and rules to guide the member nations and those adhering unilaterally to the Guidelines.

[7] Arms Export Control Act, as amended, 22 U.S.C. §§ 2751-2799aa-2.

[8] DDTC relies on other agencies, principally DOD's Defense Technology Security Administration, for technical assistance in conducting license reviews.

[9] The U.S. Munitions List provides a list of the defense articles and services that require a license for export.

[10] While DCS involves negotiations between a U.S. supplier and a foreign buyer, FMS involves negotiations between the U.S. government and a foreign government or organization.

[11] 50 U.S.C. App. §§ 2401-2420. The Export Administration Act of 1979, as amended, is not permanent legislation. Since August 21, 2001, the Export Administration Act has been in lapse. However, the President has continued the regulations in effect through Executive Order 13222 of August 17, 2001 (3 C.F.R., 2001 Comp 783 (2002)), which most recently was extended by Presidential Notice on August 12, 2011, under the authority provided by section 202(d) of the National Emergencies Act (50 U.S.C. § 1622(d)).

[12] Within BIS, Export Administration administers the license review process.

[13] Within BIS, Export Enforcement administers Commerce's end-use monitoring program.

[14] As we discuss further in this report, there is no formal mechanism to ensure that licensing agencies have relevant and timely intelligence information when making licensing decisions. For this reason, the intelligence community is not represented in figure 2.

[15] For our report, we looked at the acquisition of UAVs in terms of which countries have obtained complete UAV systems and who they had acquired those systems from. For development, we looked at which countries were building UAV systems and what they were building. The applications of UAVs addressed which tasks UAVs were performing and things that limited the tasks they were allowed to perform.

[16] GAO-04-175.

[17] We were unable to calculate a more precise figure for the military DCS licenses because of limitations in State's licensing database, which are discussed later in this report.

[18] These vehicles are commonly referred to as unmanned combat aerial vehicles.

[19] GAO, *Unmanned Aircraft Systems: Federal Actions Needed to Ensure Safety and Expand Their Potential Uses Within the National Airspace System*, GAO-08-511 (Washington, D.C.: May 15, 2008).

[20] A Special Airworthiness Certification is issued to a private entity to allow it to fly their UAV for research, training, or testing purposes. A Certificate of Authorization is provided to a federal, state, or local government entity to allow it to fly a UAV under specific conditions as part of its duties.

[21] See Defense Security Service, *Targeting U.S. Technologies* (2009).

[22] Lethal UAVs are designed to conduct one-way attacks with the vehicle being destroyed upon detonation. Weaponized UAVs are two-way attack vehicles that fly to a target, fire their munitions, and then return.

[23] A demarche is a formal diplomatic protest or representation.

[24] To conduct our analysis of the extent to which the United States used bilateral diplomacy to address UAV proliferation concerns, State provided to us copies of UAVrelated demarches. We did not conduct an independent assessment to determine whether our sample contained all the UAV-related demarches that State presented to foreign governments from January 2005 to September 2011. Appendix I provides a broad discussion of how we determined which demarches were UAV-related.

[25] The Commerce Control List is divided into 10 broad categories (categories 0 through 9), with each category containing ECCNs that describe the specific controls on a particular item or type of item.

[26] The U.S. Munitions List is divided into 21 broad categories, with each category further divided into subcategories.

[27] The majority of UAV-related dual-use and military items exported commercially require an export license from Commerce and State, respectively. Approval to transfer military UAV items through the FMS program is granted by the U.S. government through a Letter of Offer and Acceptance. DOD's DSCA manages this process, but State has final authority regarding the approval of FMS transfers.

[28] The Missile Annex Review Committee is an interagency working group led by State's Bureau of International Security and Nonproliferation. It is tasked with addressing technical issues related to the MTCR Annex. For instance, it reviews proposals for amending the Annex. At the request of groups such as the MTEC, it can also make determinations as to whether particular items are controlled by MTCR.

[29] According to State officials, Category VIII licenses are automatically assigned to DDTC's Aircraft Division; however, the DDTC's Space and Missile Technology Division is responsible for reviewing UAV-related licenses. Thus, the new procedure was designed to ensure UAV licenses were routed correctly.

[30] For Commerce's licensing data, we reported only those licenses for commodities controlled under the three UAV-specific ECCNs: 9A012, 9A120, and 9B010. Although we identified another 29 ECCNs that control commodities that could be used in UAVs, we did not report on licenses involving these commodities because they are not exclusively used in UAVs. For State's licensing data, State provided us all licenses that had gone before the MTEC over the period from fiscal years 2005 through 2010. While the majority of UAV licenses go before the MTEC, certain UAV-related licenses may not be captured within the data State provided. See appendix I for additional information about the limitations of the data and the steps we took to refine the data.

[31] In several of these cases, countries also purchased various components, parts, and accessories in addition to the systems themselves.

[32] If a license applicant fails to provide the necessary information for State to make a determination whether to approve or deny the license, State may return the application without action to the applicant.

[33] The Missile Trade Analysis Group is led by State's Bureau of International Security and Nonproliferation and includes representatives from State's Bureau of Intelligence and Research and DDTC, as well as Commerce, DOD, the Department of Energy, DHS, the FBI, the National Security Agency, and the CIA.

[34] State's DDTC administers the Blue Lantern program to monitor arms exported through DCS.

[35] DOD's DSCA administers the Golden Sentry program to monitor arms transferred through FMS.

[36] Details of this transfer are designated for official use only and are not reported here.

[37] GAO-12-89.

[38] To obtain this data on UAV-related end-use checks, State and Commerce queried their respective databases and provided us data on those end-use checks they deemed to be UAV-related over the period from fiscal years 2005 through 2010.

[39] According to State, if the critical questions have been answered satisfactorily, the transaction appears legitimate, and the *bona fides* of the end-users or other parties are confirmed, the case will likely be closed "favorable." If the transaction's legitimacy cannot be confirmed, the consignees or end-user appear untrustworthy, or if there are other troubling discrepancies, the case will likely be closed "unfavorable."

[40] According to Commerce, a check may result in a limited or inconclusive finding under a number of conditions. For instance, a check may be deemed limited if the official conducting the check cannot view the commodity in question on-site, but only the documents related to the sale, because the item was legally resold to another party. An inconclusive check may occur when the official conducting the check is unable to conclusively determine the end-use of an item because there is potentially conflicting or missing information, but there is not enough evidence to deem the check unfavorable.

[41] See GAO-12-89.

[42] See GAO-11-135R.

[43] The Export Enforcement Coordination Center includes the Departments of Commerce, Defense, Energy, Homeland Security, Justice, State, and Treasury, as well as the Office of the Director of National Intelligence.

[44] See GAO, *Export Controls: Proposed Reforms Create Opportunities to Address Enforcement Challenges,* GAO-12-246 (Washington, D.C.: Mar. 27, 2012).

[45] See GAO, *Export Controls: Challenges Exist in Enforcement of an Inherently Complex System,* GAO-07-265 (Washington, D.C.: Dec. 20, 2006).

[46] 6 Fed. Reg. 41,958, *Proposed Revisions to the Export Administration Regulations (EAR): Control of Items the President Determines No Longer Warrant Control Under the United States Munitions List* (July 15, 2011).

[47] 77 Fed. Reg. 36,409, *"Specially Designed" Definition* (June 19, 2012).

[48] This information was provided after the publication of our classified report in February 2012.

[49] The full texts of the second and third recommendations were deemed to contain sensitive information and are not included here. They are included in our February 2012 report.

End Notes for Appendix I

[1] A demarche is a formal diplomatic protest or representation.

In: Unmanned Aerial Vehicle Proliferation … ISBN: 978-1-62808-228-9
Editor: Maksim Korjus

Chapter 2

THE U.S. EXPORT CONTROL SYSTEM AND THE PRESIDENT'S REFORM INITIATIVE*

Ian F. Fergusson and Paul K. Kerr

SUMMARY

The 113th Congress may consider reforms of the U.S. export control system. The balance between national security and export competitiveness has made the subject of export controls controversial for decades. Through the Export Administration Act (EAA), the Arms Export Control Act (AECA), the International Emergency Economic Powers Act (IEEPA), and other authorities, the United States restricts the export of defense items or munitions; so-called "dual-use" goods and technology—items with both civilian and military applications; certain nuclear materials and technology; and items that would assist in the proliferation of nuclear, chemical, and biological weapons or the missile technology used to deliver them. U.S. export controls are also used to restrict exports to certain countries on which the United States imposes economic sanctions. At present, the EAA has expired and dual-use controls are maintained under IEEPA authorities.

The U.S. export control system is diffused among several different licensing and enforcement agencies. Exports of dual-use goods and technologies are licensed by the Department of Commerce, munitions are licensed by the Department of State, and restrictions on exports based on

* This is an edited, reformatted and augmented version of Congressional Research Service, Publication No. R41916, dated April 19, 2013.

U.S. sanctions are administered by the U.S. Treasury. Enforcement of export controls is conducted by these agencies as well as by units of the Department of Homeland Security (DHS) and the Department of Justice (DOJ).

Aspects of the U.S. export control system have long been criticized by exporters, nonproliferation advocates, and other stakeholders as being too rigorous, insufficiently rigorous, cumbersome, obsolete, inefficient, or any combination of these descriptions. In August 2009, the Obama Administration launched a comprehensive review of the U.S. export control system. In April 2010, Defense Secretary Robert M. Gates proposed an outline of a new system based on four singularities:

- a single export control licensing agency for both dual-use and munitions exports,
- a unified control list,
- a single enforcement coordination agency, and
- a single integrated information technology (IT) system.

The rationalization of the two control lists has been the Administration's focus to date. Interim steps have also been taken to create a single IT system and to establish an export enforcement coordination center. No specific proposals have been made concerning the single licensing agency.

In contrast to the Administration's approach, legislation was introduced to reauthorize or rewrite the EAA in the 112th Congress. The Export Administration Renewal Act of 2011 (H.R. 2122, RosLehtinen) would have renewed the currently expired Export Administration Act through 2015, updated its penalty and enforcement provisions, and provided stricter foreign policy controls on countries designated as state sponsors of terrorism. A separate title would have amended the Arms Export Control Act to permit generic parts and components for defense articles to be controlled differently than sensitive defense articles on the U.S. Munitions List. By contrast, the Technology Security Act of 2011 (H.R. 2004, Berman) would have rewritten the dual-use export control statute by giving the President the authority to control exports for national security and foreign policy reasons and to create the mechanisms for doing so. Each bill would, if passed, have implications for the President's reform efforts. In addition, the National Defense Authorization Act for FY2013 (P.L. 112-239), signed by the President on January 2, 2013, contains a provision to repeal 1998 legislation that placed commercial communications satellites (CCS) under munitions export licensing jurisdiction and to permit the President to determine the export control jurisdiction of CCS.

In considering the future of the U.S. export control system, Congress may weigh the merits of a unified export control system—the end result of the President's proposal—or the continuation of the present bifurcated system by reauthorizing the present EAA or writing new legislation. In doing so, Congress may debate the record of the present dual-use system maintained by emergency authority, the aims and effectiveness of the present non-proliferation control regimes, the maintenance of the defense industrial base, and the delicate balance between the maintenance of economic competitiveness and the preservation of national security.

OVERVIEW OF THE U.S. EXPORT CONTROL SYSTEM

The United States restricts the export of defense items or munitions; so-called "dual-use" goods and technology; certain nuclear materials and technology; and items that would assist in the development of nuclear, chemical, and biological weapons or the missile technology used to deliver them. A defense item is defined by regulation as one that is "specifically designed, developed, or configured, adapted, or modified for a military application," has neither "predominant civilian application" nor "performance equivalent to an item used for civilian application ... and has significant military or intelligence application such that control is necessary."[1] Dual-use goods are commodities, software, or technologies that have both civilian and military applications.

U.S. export controls are also used to restrict exports to certain countries on which the United States imposes economic sanctions, such as Cuba, Iran, and Syria. Through the Export Administration Act (EAA), the Arms Export Control Act (AECA), the International Emergency Economic Powers Act (IEEPA), and other authority, Congress has delegated to the executive branch its express constitutional authority to regulate foreign commerce by controlling exports. In addition, the United States controls certain exports in adherence to several multilateral nonproliferation control regimes.

Various aspects of the U.S. export control system have long been criticized by exporters, nonproliferation advocates, and other stakeholders as being too rigorous, insufficiently rigorous, cumbersome, obsolete, inefficient, or any combination of these descriptions. Some contend that U.S. export controls overly restrict U.S. exports and make firms less competitive. Others argue that U.S. defense and foreign policy considerations should trump commercial concerns. In January 2007, the Government Accountability Office (GAO) designated government programs designed to protect critical technologies, including the U.S. export control system, as a "high-risk" area "that warrants a strategic reexamination of existing programs to identify needed changes." GAO's report cited poor coordination among export control agencies, disagreements over commodity jurisdiction between the Departments of State and Commerce, unnecessary delays and inefficiencies in the license application process, and a lack of systematic evaluative mechanisms to determine the effectiveness of export controls.[2]

On August 13, 2009, President Obama announced the launch of a comprehensive review of the U.S. export control system, and this was followed in April 2010 with a speech by Secretary of Defense Robert M. Gates announcing key elements of the Administration's agenda for reform, with additional elaborations in subsequent months. Secretary Gates proposed a four-pronged approach that would establish:

- a single export control licensing agency for both dual-use and munitions exports;
- a unified control list;
- a single enforcement coordination agency; and
- a single integrated information technology system, which would include a single database of sanctioned and denied parties.

The House Committee on Foreign Affairs held its first hearing on the reform proposals on May 12, 2011. During the hearing, Chairwoman Ileana Ros-Lehtinen criticized the scope and pace of the reforms, reportedly asserting that "a compelling case has not been made for the wholesale restructuring of the current system," and that the reforms are "straining the system and its personnel to its breaking point."[3] The committee held a second hearing on February 7, 2012, to solicit private sector input.[4]

On May 26, 2011, Ranking Member Howard Berman introduced the Technology Security Act (H.R. 2004), a comprehensive rewrite of U.S. dual-use controls that would confer upon the President "broad and flexible authority to deploy controls to counteract current and future national security threats."[5] On June 3, Chairwoman Ros-Lehtinen introduced the Export Administration Renewal Act of 2011 (H.R. 2122), which would renew the currently expired Export Administration Act through 2015, amend certain other provisions of the act, and amend the Arms Export Control Act to permit differential control over parts and components on the U.S. Munitions List.

In its administration of this authority, the executive branch has created a diffuse system by which exports are controlled by differing agencies under different regulations. This section describes the characteristics of the dual-use, munitions, and nuclear controls. The information contained in this section also appears in chart form in **Appendix A**.

The Dual-Use System

The Export Administration Act (EAA)

The EAA of 1979 (P.L. 96-72) is the underlying statutory authority for dual-use export controls. The EAA, which is currently expired, periodically has been reauthorized for short periods of time. The last incremental extension expired in August 2001. At other times, and currently, the export licensing system created under the authority of the EAA has been continued by a presidential declaration of a national emergency and the invocation of the International Emergency Economic Powers Act (IEEPA; P.L. 95-223).[6] The EAA confers upon the President the power to control exports for national security, foreign policy, or short-supply purposes. It also authorizes the President to establish export licensing mechanisms for items detailed on the Commerce Control List (CCL) (see below), and it provides guidance and places certain limits on that authority.[7]

Several attempts to rewrite or reauthorize the EAA have occurred over the years. The last comprehensive effort took place during the 107th Congress. The Senate adopted legislation (S. 149) in September 2001, and a House version (H.R. 2581) was developed by the then-House International Relations Committee and the House Armed Services Committee. The full House did not act on this legislation.

The EAA, which was written and amended during the Cold War, was based on strategic relationships, perceived threats to U.S. national security, international business practices, and existing commercial technologies, many of which have changed dramatically in the past 25 years. Some Members of Congress and most U.S. business representatives see a need to liberalize U.S. export regulations to allow American companies to engage more fully in international competition for sales of high-technology goods, some of which may be commercially available from foreign competitors. Other Members and some national security analysts contend that liberalization of export controls over the past decade has contributed to foreign threats to U.S. national security, that some controls should be tightened, and that Congress should weigh further liberalization carefully.

Administration

The Bureau of Industry and Security (BIS) in the Department of Commerce administers the dual-use export control system. The export licensing and enforcement functions that now form the agency mission of BIS were detached from the International Trade Administration (ITA) in 1985 in order to separate it from the export promotion functions of that agency within the Department of Commerce. In FY2012, BIS processed 23,229 export license applications worth approximately $204.1 billion—$113.6 billion of which were licenses for crude oil exports. It denied less than 1% of license applications, although some licenses were approved with conditions. BIS was appropriated $99.7 million, including rescissions, by the Consolidated Appropriations Act (P.L. 113-6) in FY2013 with approximately 390 full-time employee positions. For FY2013, the President's budget requests $112.1 million. In addition to its export licensing and enforcement functions, BIS also enforces U.S. anti-boycott regulations concerning the Arab League boycott against Israel.

Implementing Regulations

The EAA is implemented by the Export Administration Regulations (EAR; 15 C.F.R. 730 et seq). As noted above, the EAR are continued under IEEPA's authority in times when the EAA is expired. The EAR set forth licensing policy for goods and destinations, the applications process used by exporters, and the CCL. The CCL is the list of specific goods, technologies, and software that are controlled by the EAR. The CCL is composed of 10 categories of items:

- nuclear materials, facilities, and equipment;
- materials, organisms, microorganisms, and toxins;
- materials processing;
- electronics;
- computers;
- telecommunications and information security;
- lasers and sensors;
- navigation and avionics;
- marine; and
- propulsion systems, space vehicles, and related equipment.

Each of these categories is further divided into functional groups: equipment, assemblies, and components; test, inspection, and production equipment; materials; software; and technology. Each controlled item has an export control classification number (ECCN) based on the above categories and functional groups. Each ECCN is accompanied by a description of the item and the reason for control. In addition to discrete items on the CCL, nearly all U.S.-origin commodities are "subject to the EAR." This means that any product "subject to the EAR" may be restricted to a destination based on the end-use or end-user of the product. For example, a commodity that is not on the CCL may be denied if the good is destined for a military end-use or an entity known to be engaged in weapons proliferation.

Licensing Policy

The EAR set out the licensing policy for dual-use commodities. Items are controlled for reasons of national security, foreign policy, or short supply. National security controls are based on a common multilateral control list; however, the designation of countries to which those controls are applied is based on U.S. policy. Foreign policy controls may be unilateral or multilateral in nature. Items are controlled unilaterally for anti-terrorism, regional stability, or crime control purposes. Anti-terrorism controls proscribe nearly all exports to the four countries designated as state sponsors of terrorism by the Secretary of State—Cuba, Iran, Sudan, and Syria—and North Korea. Foreign policy-based controls are also based on adherence to multilateral non-proliferation control regimes, such as the Nuclear Suppliers' Group, the Australia Group (chemical and biological precursors), and the Missile Technology Control Regime (MTCR).

The EAR set out timelines for the consideration of dual-use licenses and the process for resolving interagency disputes. Within nine days of receipt, Commerce must refer the license to other agencies (State, DOD, or the Nuclear Regulatory Commission [NRC], as appropriate), grant the license, deny it, seek additional information, or return it. If the license is referred to other agencies, the agency to which it is referred must recommend that the application be approved or denied within 30 days. The EAR provide a dispute resolution process for a dissenting agency to appeal an adverse decision. The interagency dispute resolution process is designed to be completed within 90 days. This process is depicted graphically in **Appendix B**.

Enforcement and Penalties

Because of the expiration of the EAA, current penalties for export control violations are based on those contained in IEEPA (50 U.S.C. 1701 et seq). For criminal penalties, the IEEPA sanctions individuals up to $1 million or up to

20 years imprisonment, or both, per violation (50 U.S.C. 1705(b)). Civil penalties under IEEPA are set at $250,000 per violation.

Enforcement is carried out by the Office of Export Enforcement (OEE) at BIS. OEE has a staff of approximately 170 in Washington, DC, and eight domestic field offices. OEE is authorized to carry out investigations domestically and works with DHS to conduct investigations overseas. OEE also conducts pre-license and post-shipment verification along with in-country U.S. embassy officials overseas. The Comprehensive Iran Sanctions, Accountability, and Divestment Act of 2010 (P.L. 111-195) authorized certain enforcement activities to be undertaken by the Department of Commerce pursuant to the EAA.

Military Export Controls

Arms Export Control Act (AECA)

The AECA of 1976 (P.L. 94-329) provides the President with the statutory authority for the control of defense articles and services.[8] It sets out foreign and national policy objectives for international defense cooperation and military export controls. Section 3(a) of the AECA sets forth the general criteria for countries or international organizations to be eligible to receive U.S. defense articles and defense services provided under the act. It also sets express conditions on the uses to which these defense items may be put. Section 4 of the AECA states that U.S. defense articles and defense services shall be sold to friendly countries "solely" for use in "internal security," for use in "legitimate self-defense," to enable the recipient to participate in "regional or collective arrangements or measures consistent with the Charter of the United Nations," to enable the recipient to participate in "collective measures requested by the United Nations for the purpose of maintaining or restoring international peace and security," and to enable the foreign military forces "in less developed countries to construct public works and to engage in other activities helpful to the economic and social development of such friendly countries." The AECA also contains the statutory authority for the Foreign Military Sales program, under which the U.S. government sells U.S. defense equipment, services, and training on a government-to-government basis.

Congressional Requirements

A prominent feature of the AECA is the requirement for congressional consideration of foreign arms sales proposed by the President. This procedure includes consideration of proposals to sell major defense equipment and services, or to retransfer such military items to other nations. The procedure is triggered by a formal report to Congress under Section 36 of the AECA. In general, the executive branch, after complying with the terms of the applicable section of U.S. law (usually those contained in the AECA), is free to proceed with an arms sales proposal unless Congress passes legislation prohibiting or modifying the proposed sale.

Under Section 36(b) of the ACEA, Congress must be formally notified 30 calendar days before the Administration can take the final steps to conclude a government-to-government foreign military sale or issue an export license for commercial sales of major defense equipment valued at $14 million or more, defense articles or services valued at $50 million or more, or design and construction services valued at $200 million or more. In the case of such sales to NATO member states Japan, Australia, or New Zealand, Congress must be formally notified 15 calendar days before the Administration can proceed with the sale. However, the prior notice thresholds are higher for Japan, Australia, and New Zealand. These higher thresholds are $25 million for the sale, enhancement, or upgrading of major defense equipment; $100 million for the sale, enhancement, or upgrading of defense articles and defense services; and $300 million for the sale, enhancement, or upgrading of design and construction services, so long as such sales to these countries do not include or involve sales to a country outside of this group of nations.

Licensing Policy

The International Traffic in Arms Regulations (ITAR) set out licensing policy for exports (and some temporary imports) of U.S. Munitions List (USML) items. A license is required for the export of nearly all items on the USML. Canada has a limited exemption, as it is considered part of the U.S. defense industrial base. In addition, the United States has recently signed treaties with the United Kingdom and Australia to exempt certain defense articles from licensing obligations to approved end-users in those countries. These treaties were ratified by the Senate in 2010. Unlike some Commerce Department dual-use controls, licensing requirements are based on the nature of the article and not the end-use or end-user of the item. The United States prohibits munitions exports to countries either unilaterally or based on adherence to United Nations (U.N.) arms embargoes. In addition, any firm engaged in manufacturing, exporting, or brokering any item on the USML must register with the Directorate of Defense Trade Controls (DDTC) at the State Department and pay a yearly fee, which is currently on a sliding scale between $2,250 and $2,750, whether or not it seeks to export during the year.

Administration

Exports of defense goods and services are administered by the Directorate of Defense Trade Controls (DDTC) at the Department of State. DDTC is a component of the Bureau of Political-Military Affairs and consists of four offices: Management, Policy, Licensing, and Compliance. In FY2012, DDTC is being funded at a level of $11.6 million. It has a staff of 81 and it completed action on 82,095 export license applications in FY2011. DDTC's FY2013 budget request is for $9.4 million, a reduction primarily due to the proposed use of fees to fund compliance personnel.

Critics of the defense trade system have long decried the delays and backlogs in processing license applications at DDTC. A National Security Presidential Directive (NSPD-56), signed by President Bush on January 22, 2008, directed that the review and adjudication of defense trade licenses submitted under ITAR are to be completed within 60 days, except where certain national security exemptions apply. Previously, except for the congressional notification procedures discussed above, DDTC had no defined timeline for the application process. The average license processing time was 18 days in FY2011. As a result of National Security Council guidelines implemented in June 2009, processing times for resolving commodity jurisdiction cases—another area of concern for GAO in its "high-risk" report—had been reduced to 36 days in 2010 from 112 in 2002.[9]

Enforcement and Penalties

The AECA provides for criminal penalties of up to $1 million or 10 years of imprisonment, or both, for each violation. The AECA also authorizes civil penalties of up to $500,000 and debarment from future exports. DDTC has a small enforcement staff (19 in the Office of Defense Trade Compliance) and works with the Defense Security Service and the Customs and Border Protection (CBP) and Immigration and Customs Enforcement (ICE) units at the Department of Homeland Security (DHS). DDTC assists DHS and the Department of Justice (DOJ) in pursuing criminal investigations and prosecutions. DDTC also coordinates the Blue Lantern end-use monitoring program, in which in-country U.S. embassy officials conduct pre-license checks and post-shipment verifications.

Nuclear Controls

A subset of the above-mentioned dual-use and military controls are controls on nuclear items and technology. Controls on nuclear goods and technology are derived from the Atomic Energy Act of 1954, as amended, and the Nuclear Non-proliferation Act of 1978, as well as from the EAA and the AECA. Controls on nuclear exports are divided among several agencies, based on the product or service being exported. The Nuclear Regulatory Commission (NRC) regulates exports of nuclear facilities and material. The NRC licensing policy and control list are located at 10 C.F.R. 110. BIS licenses "outside the core" civilian power plant equipment and maintains the Nuclear Referral List as part of the CCL. The Department of Energy licenses the export of nuclear technology. DDTC exercises licensing authority over nuclear items in defense articles under the ITAR.

Defense Technology Security Administration (DTSA)

DTSA is located in the Department of Defense, Office of the Under Secretary of Defense for Policy under the Assistant Secretary of Defense for Global Security Affairs.

DTSA coordinates the technical and national security review of direct commercial sales export licenses and commodity jurisdiction requests received from the Departments of Commerce and State. It develops the recommendation of DOD on these referred export licenses or commodity jurisdictions based on input provided by the various DOD departments and agencies and represents DOD in the interagency dispute resolution process. Not all licenses from DDTC or BIS are referred to DTSA; memorandums of understanding govern the types of licenses referred from each agency. DTSA coordinates the DOD position with regard to proposed changes to the ITAR and the EAR. It also represents DOD in the interagency process responsible for compliance with multinational export control regimes.

Enforcement of U.S. Export Controls

Enforcement of the U.S. export control system is undertaken by the agencies responsible for export licensing, the Department of Homeland Security (DHS), the Department of Justice (DOJ) (National Security Division and the Federal Bureau of Investigation [FBI]), and the Defense Criminal Investigative Service. Their activities can be summarized as follows:

- **Office of Export Enforcement (OEE) at the Bureau of Industry and Security (BIS).** OEE investigates violations of the dual-use export control regime. OEE is authorized to conduct domestic investigations and works with the Immigration and Customs Enforcement Agency (ICE) of DHS on investigations of export control violations overseas. OEE refers civil violations to the Office of Chief Counsel at BIS and criminal violations to DOJ.
- **Office of Defense Trade Compliance (ODTC) at the Directorate of Defense Trade Controls (DDTC).** ODTC primarily administers internal civil enforcement actions, including charging letters and consent agreements, policies of denial, debarments, transaction exceptions, and reinstatements. ODTC provides agency support to investigations and criminal enforcement actions primarily conducted by ICE and the FBI.
- **Office of Enforcement, Nuclear Regulatory Commission (NRC).** Investigates export control violations of nuclear facilities and material licensed by the NRC's Office of International Programs. The Office of Enforcement refers criminal violations to DOJ.
- **Immigration and Customs Enforcement (ICE) of DHS.** As with its predecessor at the U.S. Customs Service, ICE has been the lead agency for export enforcement activities. The Counter-Proliferation Investigations (CPI) Unit investigates violations of dual-use and munitions export controls, exports to sanctioned countries, and violations of economic embargoes. ICE supplements and provides enforcement capacity to the export licensing agencies (BIS and DDTC) and undertakes investigations based on its own and other agency intelligence. In addition, export controls are enforced at the port of departure by DHS Customs and Border Protection.
- **National Security Division of DOJ.** The counter-espionage section of this division undertakes criminal prosecutions resulting from investigations conducted by the licensing agencies, ICE, and the FBI. An October 2007 DOJ National Export Enforcement Initiative established task forces between the licensing and enforcement agencies and U.S. Attorney's Offices in 20 cities to coordinate export control prosecutions and has facilitated new counter-proliferation

coordination among law enforcement agencies, export licensing agencies, and the intelligence community.

- **Federal Bureau of Investigation (FBI).** The FBI's Weapons of Mass Destruction Directorate receives and analyzes intelligence regarding proliferation networks, provides specialized training on counter-proliferation for the National Export Enforcement Initiative, and cooperates with above-mentioned investigative partners and export licensing agencies.
- **Defense Criminal Investigation Service (DCIS).** DCIS is the criminal investigative arm of the Inspector General of DOD. Among its varied activities, DCIS investigates the transfer of sensitive defense technologies to proscribed nations and criminal elements.

Multilateral Control Regimes

In addition to U.S. controls, there are four major multilateral control regimes: the Australia Group, the Missile Technology Control Regime, the Nuclear Suppliers Group, and the Wassenaar Arrangement.[10] The Commerce Department observed on December 9, 2010, that "[m]ost items on the CCL are controlled in accordance with the United States' commitments" to four major multilateral export control regimes.[11]

In addition to the controls described in the box below, all of these regimes have catch-all controls, which allow for the control of non-listed items if they are to be used for a military or proliferation-related purpose.

Multilateral Control Regimes

Australia Group: a voluntary, informal, export control arrangement founded in 1985 and consisting of 41 members. It has a set of export guidelines, as well as six common control lists. These lists include dual-use chemical manufacturing and biological equipment, chemical weapons precursors, and biological agents.

Missile Technology Control Regime (MTCR): an informal voluntary export control arrangement established in 1987. The 34 members of the regime agree to adhere to common export policy guidelines applied to lists of controlled items.

The MTCR guidelines call on each partner country to exercise restraint when considering transfers of equipment or technology, as well as “intangible” transfers, that would provide, or help a recipient country build, a missile capable of delivering a 500 kilogram warhead to a range of 300 kilometers or more. The MTCR annex contains two categories of controlled items. Category I items are the most sensitive. There is “a strong presumption to deny” such transfers, according to the MTCR guidelines. Regime partners have greater flexibility with respect to exports of Category II items.

Nuclear Suppliers Group (NSG): an informal association of nuclear exporters founded in 1975 and currently consisting of 46 members. NSG members voluntarily agree to coordinate exports of civilian nuclear material, as well as nuclear-related equipment and technology, to non-nuclear-weapon states.[12] The group’s guidelines include lists of materials and equipment subject to export control, in addition to requiring importers to offer nonproliferation and physical security assurances.

Wassenaar Arrangement: a voluntary export control regime approved in 1996 and currently consisting of 40 members. Its participants agree to control exports and retransfers of items on a munitions list and a list of dual-use goods and technologies. According to its Guidelines and Procedures, the Wassenaar Arrangement is not formally targeted at “any state or group of states,” but is designed “to contribute to regional and international security and stability, by promoting transparency and greater responsibility in transfers of conventional arms and dual-use goods and technologies, thus preventing destabilizing accumulations.” Participants exchange information regarding transfers and licenses for items covered by the arrangement.

Because, as noted, the Export Administration Act (EAA) has expired, there is only one law in force explicitly requiring the U.S. government to adhere to a multilateral export control regime. The Arms Export Control Act requires the Secretary of State to maintain, as part of the U.S. Munitions List, “a list of all items on the MTCR Annex” that are not controlled pursuant to the EAA. The Atomic Energy Act requires the executive branch to control nuclear-related items, but the law does not explicitly require that these items be the same as those controlled by the Nuclear Suppliers Group.

THE PRESIDENT'S EXPORT CONTROL INITIATIVE

On August 13, 2009, President Obama announced the launch of a comprehensive review of the U.S. export control system. Defense Secretary Robert M. Gates announced key elements of the Administration's agenda for reform in a speech on April 20, 2010, with additional elaborations in subsequent months. Secretary Gates proposed a four-pronged approach that would create a single export control licensing agency for both dual-use and munitions exports; adopt a unified control list; establish a single enforcement coordination agency; and create a single integrated information technology system, which would include a single database of sanctioned and denied parties.

The Administration's blueprint envisioned that these changes would be implemented in three phases, with the final phase requiring legislative action. In Phase I, preparatory work would be undertaken to harmonize the Commerce Control List (CCL) with the U.S. Munitions List (USML). Standardized licensing processes among the control agencies would be developed, and an "Enforcement Fusion Center" to synchronize enforcement would be created along with a single electronic gateway to access the licensing system. Phase II would implement a harmonized licensing system with two identically structured tiered control lists, potentially allowing for a reduction in the amount of licenses required by the system. Certain items could be moved from the USML to the CCL, for which congressional notification would be required; unilateral controls on certain items would be examined; and consultations would take place with multilateral control regime partners to add or remove multilateral controls on certain items.

Under the proposal, the new export control system would debut in Phase III. A single licensing agency would be established; the two harmonized, tiered control lists would be merged with mechanisms for review and updating; and a single IT system for licensing and enforcement would become operational. Also, an Export Enforcement Coordination Center, which was created by executive order on November 9, 2010, would be housed and funded by the Department of Homeland Security. Changes in agency structure may require legislation and may be proposed in the 112th Congress.

In a February 2011 speech, BIS Assistant Secretary Kevin Wolf elucidated seven principles driving the Administration's export control reform efforts:

- Controls should focus on a small core set of key items that can pose a serious national security or intelligence threat to the United States and its interests.
- Controls should be fully coordinated with the multilateral export control regimes in order to be effective.
- Unilateral controls must address an existing legal or foreign policy objective.
- Control lists must clearly identify which items are controlled and be easily updated as technology emerges, matures, or becomes widely available.
- Licensing processes must be predictable and timely.
- Enforcement capabilities must be enhanced to address non-compliance and increase capacity to interdict unapproved transfers.
- Controls must address counterterrorism policy and the need to export items that support homeland security priorities.[13]

The Four Singularities

A Single Licensing Agency

In his speech introducing the Administration's reform efforts, Secretary Gates described the bureaucratic structure of the U.S. export control system as a "byzantine amalgam of authorities, roles, and missions scattered around different parts of the federal government."[14] As noted above, licensing is divided among the Department of Commerce for dual-use items, the Department of State for munitions, the Department of the Treasury for certain sanctions, and the Nuclear Regulatory Commission and Department of Energy for certain nuclear materials and technologies. These entities operate under different statutory authorities and enforce different regulations. While there are mechanisms in place for license referrals and to address licensing disagreements, critics have long maintained that the multi-agency structure contributes to institutional squabbling among the different agencies responsible for export control licensing. Having one licensing system would also end disputes about commodity jurisdiction over a given item.

On June 30, 2010, then-National Security Adviser General Jim Jones announced that the Administration intended to create an independent licensing agency with Cabinet members from existing control agencies serving as a board of directors. While the Administration has not proffered specific details about this new agency, it is expected to take over the licensing functions of

BIS, DDTC, and OFAC. Civil and administrative enforcement functions of BIS and DDTC are likely to be housed in the new unified licensing agency. Licensing procedures of the NRC for nuclear materials and of the Department of Energy for technology will not be moved. According to an Administration official, this is due to the relatively small volume of licensing undertaken for nuclear materials as well as by the small universe of exporters.[15]

Table 1. President's Export Control Reform Initiative

Phase	Control List	Licensing	Enforcement	Information Technology
I	Refine, understand, harmonize definitions to end jurisdictional confusion between two lists; establish new control criteria	Implement regulatory-based improvements to streamline licensing	Synchronize and de-conflict enforcement; create Enforcement Fusion Center	Determine enterprise-wide needs
II (requires congressional notification; requires additional funding)	Restructure two lists into identical tiered structures; apply criteria; remove unilateral controls where appropriate; submit proposals multilaterally to add/remove controls	Complete transition to mirrored control list, fully implement licensing harmonization	Expand outreach and compliance	Transition toward a single electronic licensing system
III (requires legislation)	Merge two lists into a single list; implement process for updating list	Implement single licensing agency	Consolidate enforcement activities under one agency	Implement a single system for licensing and enforcement

Source: Prepared by Dianne Rennack, CRS, based on White House Fact Sheet, April 20, 2010.

One rationale advanced by General Jones is that a unified licensing structure would end the stovepipe situation whereby no agency collectively knows what has been licensed (or denied) by the U.S. government. Under current referral processes, dual-use licenses are referred by BIS to the Department of Defense, the Department of State (Economic Energy and Business Bureau [EEB], International Security and Non-Proliferation [ISN] Bureau, and the regional bureaus), and in some instances to the Treasury's

Office of Foreign Assets Control (OFAC) for review. However, Department of Commerce licenses are not referred to DDTC. DDTC refers munitions licenses to DOD and to the above-mentioned bureaus at State, but not to Commerce. OFAC licenses are referred only to State's EEB. As a result, situations have arisen whereby licenses requested by the same exporter to the same destination have been approved by one license agency and denied by another.

While a single licensing agency may do away with the stovepipe issue, the envisioned single information technology system (see below) among the current agencies may also address this problem. In addition, licenses would still need to be referred to other bureaus at State and DOD, so interagency policy differences may continue to exist.

Dual-Nationals

One example of the effort that will be necessary to create a unified export control system may be seen in the dual-national issue. The White House announced on March 11, 2010, that it would take action to eliminate "obstacles to exporting to companies employing dual nationals." Specifically, the Administration announced that it would "begin to harmonize" conflicting standards used by the Departments of Commerce and State to determine a foreign person's nationality—a step that these departments must take in order to make certain export control decisions.[16] The Commerce Department, according to a 2010 Government Accountability Office (GAO) report, determines "nationality for release of technology to a foreign national" based on that person's "most recent citizenship or permanent residence."[17]

The State Department, however, considers not only a foreign national's current citizenship status, but also their country of birth if it differs from the person's country of citizenship or permanent residency. Even if a foreign entity is approved for a manufacturing license agreement or a technical assistance agreement with a U.S. firm, the State Department must approve the transfer of technical data, defense services, and defense articles to dual nationals and third-party nationals employed by the foreign entity.[18] "If a person's country of birth is prohibited from receiving U.S. arms, as are China, Iran, and North Korea, State collects additional information to confirm that the individual has no significant ties to his or her country of birth," according to the GAO.

Both the State Department and private-sector experts argue that these requirements are contentious because, in addition to being administratively burdensome, they are a potential employment discrimination issue in other countries; in order to comply with the regulations, nonU.S. employers may need to limit employment opportunities in potential violation of their countries' employment laws.[19]

After publishing a proposed rule on August 11, 2010,[20] the State Department published a final rule on May 16, 2011, that would amend the ITAR to allow the transfer of defense articles and technical data to dual or third-party nationals who are "bona fide, regular employees, directly employed by the foreign consignee or end-user."[21] Such transfers

> must take place completely within the physical territory of the country where the end-user is located, where the governmental entity or international organization conducts official business, or where the consignee operates, and be within the scope of an approved export license, other export authorization, or license exemption.

The end user or consignee must take a variety of measures designed to prevent the diversion of any exports; the final rule includes a requirement for the end user to screen employees for "substantive contacts with restricted or prohibited countries" listed in the ITAR.[22] The rule, which became effective on August 15, 2011, also explains that, although "nationality does not, in and of itself, prohibit access to defense articles or defense services, an employee that has substantive contacts" with persons from prohibited countries "shall be presumed to raise a risk of diversion," unless the State Department determines otherwise.

It is worth noting that, according to the State Department, "most diversions of U.S. Munitions List ... items appear to occur outside the scope of approved licenses, not within foreign companies or organizations providing access to properly screened dual national or third country national employees."[23]

The Single Control List

To date, the Administration has concentrated on rationalizing the control lists to form the basis from which other reforms will flow. The Administration first seeks to transform the current USML from a "negative list" characterized by general descriptions of articles and design-intentbased criteria to one resembling the current CCL, a "positive" list of dual-use items that are controlled according to objective criteria or parameters. This is being done through the so-called "bright line" process to determine which items should be controlled as dual-use goods and which should be controlled as munitions. The bright line is being determined at the commodity level, based on technical specification and military needs, and is not an overarching concept or framework. The Administration describes the bright line as necessary, in part, because of the USML's current reliance on design intent (i.e., whether an item was "specifically designed, modified, or adapted" for military use) and its catch-all controls of parts and components of these items.[24] While the CCL is described as more "positive," it too contains entries containing the term "specially designed" for a specific purpose that may need to be modified to conform to bright line standards.

Originally, each of the items on the resulting USML list was to have been assigned to a tier to determine its level of control. The Administration created three tiers applicable to both the CCL and the USML to categorize a different level of control.[25] However, the tiering process was dropped, reportedly because it would have been necessary to decide on the tiers for all USML items prior to publishing any revised USML categories, which the Administration has proceeded to do on a rolling basis.[26] While the tiering process may have been dropped for the revision process, it still may be used to differentiate items on the USML and CCL or under a future merged list if the revision process is completed.

Each category of the USML is being screened by an interagency team led by DOD, and proposed revisions to each USML category, including certain items proposed to be moved to the CCL, are being published as proposed rulemakings. Proposed revisions to Category IV (launch vehicles, missiles, rockets, torpedoes, bombs, mines, and other military explosive devices); (Category V (Explosives and Energetic Materials, Propellants, Incendiary Agents and Their Constituents); Category VI (vessels of war and naval equipment); Category VII (tanks and military vehicles);

Category IX (Military Training Equipment); Category X (Protective Personal Equipment and Shelters); Category XI (military electronics); Category XIII (auxiliary military equipment); and Category XX (submersible vessels and oceanic equipment) have been published in the Federal Register since 2011. Final rules on the migration of items in Category VIII (aircraft and associated equipment) and a new Category XIX (gas turbine engines) were issued on April 16, 2013.[27] (See **Appendix D** for the status of current proposals to move certain items from the USML to the CCL.) A final rule on a new "OY521" classification series has also been issued. The OY521 series will be used for items that the U.S. government determines warrant control due to a significant military or intelligence advantage it would confer or due to foreign policy reasons, but are not identified under an existing ECCN, nor are controlled under an existing U.S. or multilateral framework.[28]

According to Administration thinking, the USML will contain "only those items that provide at least a significant military or intelligence applicability that warrant the controls the AECA requires."[29] The reconstituted Munitions List may then be aligned with the CCL by adopting its A-E commodity organization structure and adding two additional categories: F and G for ITAR specific controls. As a result of this alignment, each USML category will be divided into seven groups: A—equipment, assemblies, and components; B—test, inspection, and production equipment; C—materials; D—software; E—technology; F—defense services; and G— manufacturing and production authorizations.

"600 Series"

As a result of the revision process, the Administration likely will seek to move some USML items to the CCL. Under Section 38(f) of the Arms Export Control Act (P.L. 90-629), the President may not remove any article from the USML until 30 days after providing notice to the House Foreign Affairs Committee, and the Senate Foreign Relations Committee, including a description of the nature of any subsequent controls on the item. The Administration issued its first notifications to Congress for Category VIII (aircraft and associated equipment) and Category XIX (Gas Turbine Engines) on March 8, 2013.

In order to comply with Section 38(f), the manner in which USML items transferred to the CCL are to be controlled is described in a proposed rulemaking on July 15, 2011.[30] It involves the creation of a "600 Series" subcategory of Export Control Classification Numbers (ECCNs) for each category on the CCL.[31] This new series will be populated by items that are judged not to need the relatively stricter controls mandated under the USML. Items moved to the CCL in this manner will require a license to all destinations except Canada. All items controlled pursuant to multilateral control regimes would retain their existing controls. In addition, "600 Series" items will be subject to a general policy of denial to countries subject to a U.S. or U.N. arms embargo.

The proposed rule also places restrictions on the extent to which certain license exceptions can be applied. End-use items transferred to the 600 Series would be eligible for the recently announced Strategic Trade Authorization (STA) license exception (described below) only after a determination is jointly made by the State, Defense, and Commerce Departments that a license exception should be made available for the item in question. Parts, components, and accessories transferred under this process would be automatically eligible for an STA license exception for exports to the governments of STA-eligible countries. "600 Series" items would also be eligible for other preexisting license exceptions.

The status of parts and components is another issue that is addressed by the "600 Series." Under the EAR, the license requirement is based on the finished product, generally without regard to its parts and components. However, a foreign product containing more than 25% U.S. content (10% U.S. content in the case of a transaction to a country identified as a state sponsor of terrorism) may require a reexport license from the United States. However, for ITAR-controlled items, DDTC has employed a jurisdictional interpretation known as a "see-through" rule, which may require U.S. reexport controls on parts and components incorporated into end products manufactured overseas.[32] For items migrating to the 600 Series, a 10% rule will apply.

"Specially Designed"

To facilitate the transfer of items from the USML to the CCL, the Administration has proposed a new definition of "specially designed." As noted above, the Administration has sought to move away from the design-intent standard of the USML and the use of the catch-all phrase "specifically designed" for military use to subject parts and components to ITAR jurisdiction. The new definition was seen as necessary given that "specifically designed" in the USML did not have the same meaning as the term "specially designed" which appears in the CCL and also in various multilateral control lists. It was also seen as infeasible to remove the term(s) entirely by enumerating each part and component being moved from the USML to the CCL.

After two previous iterations, the Administration published its final rulemaking on the definition of "specially designed" on April 16, 2013. [33] The two-part definition has been dubbed a "catch and release" approach in that the first part of the definition may capture and item as specially designed for military use and the second part may release the item from control under the definition if it does not qualify under certain parameters. Under the first part of the regulation, an item qualifies as specially designed if:

> (1) As a result of "development" has properties peculiarly responsible for achieving or exceeding the performance levels, characteristics, or functions in the relevant ECCN or U.S. Munitions List (USML) paragraph; or

(2) Is a "part," "component," "accessory," "attachment," or "software" for use in or with a commodity or defense article 'enumerated' or otherwise described on the CCL or the USML.

Under the proposed regulation, if none of the two above criteria apply to an item, then the item is not specially designed. If one or more of these criteria describes an item, it potentially qualifies it as specially designed and is subject to the following six exclusions, any one of which would exclude the item from being specially designed:

(1) Has been identified to be in an ECCN paragraph that does not contain "specially designed" as a control parameter or as an EAR99 item in a commodity jurisdiction (CJ) determination or interagency-cleared commodity classification (CCATS);
(2) Is, regardless of 'form' or 'fit,' a fastener (*e.g.*, screw, bolt, nut, nut plate, stud, insert, clip, rivet, pin), washer, spacer, insulator, grommet, bushing, spring, wire, solder;
(3) Has the same function, performance capabilities, and the same or 'equivalent' form and fit, as a commodity or software used in or with an item that:
    (i) Is or was in "production" (*i.e.*, not in "development"); *and*
    (ii) Is either not 'enumerated' on the CCL or USML, or is described in an ECCN controlled only for Anti-Terrorism (AT) reasons;
(4) Was or is being developed with "knowledge" that it would be for use in or with commodities or software (i) described in an ECCN *and* (ii) also commodities or software either not 'enumerated' on the CCL or the USML (e.g., EAR99 commodities or software) or commodities or software described in an ECCN controlled only for Anti-Terrorism (AT) reasons;
(5) Was or is being developed as a general purpose commodity or software, i.e., with no "knowledge" for use in or with a particular commodity (e.g., an F/A-18 or HMMWV) or type of commodity (e.g., an aircraft or machine tool); *or*
(6) Was or is being developed with "knowledge" that it would be for use in or with commodities or software described (i) in an ECCN controlled for AT-only reasons and also EAR99 commodities or software; or (ii) exclusively for use in or with EAR99 commodities or software."[34]

Under this decision tree approach, the item is potentially "caught" as specially designed by the first two criteria, but it may be "released" from that definition if any of the six subsequent qualifiers apply. The Commerce regulations would apply to the "600 series" of items moved from the USML. The proposed regulation to define specially designed in the ITAR as a replacement for the currently utilized "specifically designed" is similar in nature. The final rule for this was published on April 16, 2013.[35]

In a speech on July 17, 2012, BIS Assistant Secretary Kevin Wolf acknowledged that the specially designed concept is "inherently difficult to apply in reality," and that it is "not consistent with the "ultimate goal of creating a truly positive, objective list of controlled items."[36] However, he noted that concurrent with this approach, BIS also published an advanced notice of proposed rulemaking (ANPR) in June 2012 seeking comments on the feasibility of enumerating or positively identifying each item determined classified as specially designed on the CCL.[37]

Strategic Trade Authorization License Exception

In 2011, the Administration devised a new license exception known as the Strategic Trade Authorization (STA), which is designed to facilitate transfers to low risk countries and to promote interoperability to allies in the field.[38] To be eligible, exporters would have to provide notification to BIS of the transaction and a destination control statement notifying the foreign consignee of the terms of the exception's safeguard requirements, and they must obtain from the foreign consignee a statement acknowledging its understanding and willingness to comply with the requirements of the license exception.

Under the final rulemaking, STA would be available in various degrees to 44 countries. To a group of 36 countries made up of NATO partners and members of all 4 multilateral nonproliferation control regimes, dual-use items controlled for national security (NS), chemical or biological weapons, nuclear non-proliferation, regional stability, crime control, or significant items (hot section jet technology) would be eligible for an STA. This would include almost all items on the CCL that are not controlled for statutory reasons. An additional eight countries would be eligible for exports, reexports, or transfers controlled for NS-only and that are not designated as STA-excluded.[39]

Dual-use items controlled for missile technology (MT), chemical weapons (CW), short supply (SS), or surreptitiously listening (SL) would not be eligible for export under STA. Certain implements of execution and torture, pathogens and toxins, software and technology for "hot-sections" of aero gas-turbine engines, and encryption have also been excluded from the STA. According to former Commerce Secretary Locke, the license exception will eliminate the need for licenses for over 3,000 yearly types of transactions, affecting $1.4 billion in exports.[40]

Commercial Communications Satellites

Although most items on either the CCL or the USML were placed there by executive discretion or by international agreement, one category of items is on the USML by statute: commercial communications satellites (CCS). Prior to 1990, CCS were controlled exclusively by the Department of State under the authority of Section 38 of the Arms Export Control Act (P.L. 90-629). Despite having both military and civilian uses, CCS were considered munitions, as many satellites and associated technologies were originally designed "specifically" for military purposes and continue to have "significant military or intelligence applications as defined by regulation." In 1990, however, President George H. W. Bush ordered a review of dual-use items, including CCS, on the U.S. Munitions List (USML), which resulted in satellites without military performance characteristics being moved to Department of Commerce jurisdiction. In 1996, President Clinton transferred all CCS (along with commercial jet "hot section" technology) to Commerce jurisdiction with enhanced licensing procedures. Following 1998 revelations by the Cox Committee that U.S. satellite manufacturers provided missile design information and skills to China through the improper transfer of launch failure analysis, Congress passed legislation transferring the authority, effective March 15, 1999, to license exports of CCS to the Department of State (P.L. 105-261).

The satellite industry claims that this transfer has led to licensing delays and lost sales resulting from regulatory uncertainty, and it has lobbied to revert export controls to Commerce Department jurisdiction. Satellites launched for commercial communication purposes may contain embedded sensitive technology, such as positioning thrusters, signal encryption, mating and separation mechanisms, and multiple satellite/reentry vehicle systems, which as standalone items are also controlled under the USML. Industry claims that because of State's "see-through" policy of requiring licenses for parts and components embedded in CCS, foreign satellite manufacturers are designing out U.S. parts and components and advertising them as ITAR-free (i.e., free of munitions licensing requirements).

In addition, Tiananmen Square sanctions and other waiver restrictions have precluded U.S. exports to China, a competitive launch destination.

Section 1248 of the 2010 National Defense Authorization Act (P.L. 111-84) directed the Secretaries of State and Defense to conduct a review of U.S. space export control policy, including a risk assessment of removing satellite and related components from the USML. An interim assessment, which was reported to Congress in May 2011, found that CCS, related components, and integration and launch information "with certain exceptions, conditions and limitations" could be removed from the USML and transferred to the CCL "without posing an unacceptable security risk." The final review, which was delivered to Congress on April 18, 2012, recommended that Congress should return export control jurisdiction for CCS to presidential discretion, as well as to authorize the Department of Defense to determine the need for special export control monitoring and oversight services for CCS and authorize DOD to be reimbursed for those services.

The National Defense Authorization Act of 2013 (P.L. 112-239), contains language (§1261) to repeal the 1999 NDAA provision transferring "satellites and related items" to the USML, potentially allowing the President to transfer satellites and related items to the CCL with certain country restrictions and reporting requirements. It would continue the prohibition on satellite sales to or launches by China, or to countries designated as state sponsors of terrorism (Cuba, Iran, Sudan, Syria) and North Korea. In addition, a license application to export satellites and related items to a country in which the United States maintains a comprehensive arms embargo will face a presumption of denial, although not an outright prohibition. The Administration may seek such legislation as it determines which items to migrate on Category XV (space systems) from the USML to the CCL.

The Single Enforcement Structure

The third singularity involves the creation of a streamlined export enforcement system. Under Phase I of the new approach, a single export "fusion center" would be created to "coordinate and de-conflict investigations, serve as a central point of contact for coordinating export control enforcement with Intelligence Community activities, and synchronize overlapping outreach programs."[41] On November 9, 2010, the Obama Administration issued Executive Order 13558, which created the Export Enforcement Coordination Center (EECC). The center officially opened in March 2012 within the

Department of Homeland Security and carries on the functions of the existing National Export Enforcement Coordination Network (NEECN) in ICE. It consists of a director from the Department of Homeland Security and two deputies appointed from the Departments of Commerce and Justice, with an intelligence community liaison designated by the Director of National Intelligence.

The center functions as the primary forum to coordinate export control enforcement efforts among the Departments of State, the Treasury, Commerce, Defense, Justice, Energy, and Homeland Security and the Director of National Intelligence and to resolve potential conflicts in criminal and administrative export control enforcement. The center is also able to screen all license applications. Previously, the OEE at BIS was the only entity that could screen dual-use licenses, whereas ICE could screen licenses from DDTC and OFAC. The unit will also establish government-wide statistical tracking capabilities for criminal and administrative enforcement activities. Also in March 2012, an Information Triage Unit was established in the Department of Commerce to serve as an information gathering and screening unit among law enforcement agencies, the intelligence community, and the export licensing agencies. The unit is designed to serve as a central point to disseminate relevant information for each license application prior to decisionmaking.[42]

The EECC is not to be confused with the National Export Control Coordinator, housed in the Justice Department, which is "responsible for ensuring full coordination between the Justice Department and the many other US law enforcement, licensing, and intelligence agencies that play a role in export enforcement."[43] The role of the coordinator has been described as the chief prosecutor of export control enforcement with the authority to determine which cases to bring for criminal prosecution.

In Phase III, the Administration may request the movement of the BIS Office of Export Enforcement to ICE. Currently, ICE conducts investigations and criminal enforcement for DDTC and OFAC, and by virtue of its authority under the IEEPA, it shares dual-use investigations with OEE. Removal of OEE to ICE will end this overlap of authority. It is envisioned that the Phase III consolidated licensing agency will continue to have authority over administrative enforcement actions.[44]

A Single Information Technology System

The fourth singularity is the creation of a single information technology system to be used to administer the export control system. The USXPORTS database, currently used by the Department of Defense to track license applications referred to it, is being expanded to State and Commerce. When completed, it will become the platform for a proposed single export license application form to be used by State, Commerce, and the Treasury's Office of Foreign Assets Control. It will also be used by the Department of Energy, Immigration and Customs Enforcement, and the Export Coordination Enforcement Center. The new system was reportedly still being tested in December 2012.[45]

This reform is being proposed to streamline the interagency review process. Currently, the agencies' computer systems are not compatible and cannot seamlessly share licensing application information with referring agencies. OFAC uses a paper-based licensing system. BIS, in particular, has had difficulties in securing its system, which was hacked in late 2006. In response, BIS completed a replacement of all its computers in 2010—a step that will help prepare it for the adoption of the single IT system.[46]

The Administration's plan calls for the adoption of USXPORTS first for internal communications such as license referrals, while exporters would continue to use the existing SNAP-R and D-Trade electronic license filing portals. Currently, a license submitted to BIS using the SNAP-R system must be converted to BIS's internal ECASS system for internal deliberation, and if sent for referral, it must be converted to the USXPORTS (for Defense) or D-Trade (for State).[47] The Administration has indicated that eventually it would like to facilitate interoperability between the license portals, the internal systems, and Customs' Automated Export System (AES), the information system that tracks actual movement of goods.

In conjunction with the single IT system, the Administration is developing a single license application form. To make this possible, the Administration is grappling with standardizing certain definitions between the different regulations, such as the use of the term "technology" in the EAR as opposed to the term "technical data" used in the ITAR.[48]

To assist in compliance with U.S. export regulations, BIS has also compiled a consolidated screening list of over 24,000 entities from existing Commerce, Treasury, and State Department screening lists. The list consolidates the BIS Denied Person List, Unverified List, and Entity List; the Department of State's Nonproliferation Sanctions List; the Directorate of Defense Trade Controls Debarred List; and the Office of Foreign Assets Control Specially Designated Nationals List.

Encryption

While not announced as part of the four singularities, reform of encryption controls has been proposed as one of the first deliverables in the export control reform process. The Administration announced on March 11, 2010, that it would change a filing requirement for exporters of products with encryption capabilities. At the time, exporters of such products were required to file for a technical review by the Commerce Department, a process that, according to the White House announcement, could take "between 30-60 days." The announcement advocated replacing this process with "a more efficient one-time notification-and-ship process," which would ensure that the "U.S. government still receives information it needs for its national security requirements while facilitating U.S. exports and innovation for new products and new technologies."[49]

The Commerce Department announced on June 25, 2010, that it was amending the Export Administration Regulations (EAR) as "the first step in the President's effort to reform U.S. encryption export controls."[50] As described by the Commerce Department's Bureau of Industry and Security, the amendment to the EAR includes[51]

- replacing, for encryption products "of lesser national security concern," the "30- day waiting requirement for a technical review" with a "provision that allows immediate authorization to export and reexport these products" after the exporter submits an electronic encryption registration to BIS;
- similarly replacing the 30-day requirement for most mass-market encryption products;[52]
- an "overarching note to exclude particular products that use cryptography from being controlled as 'information security' items"—a measure that implements changes approved by the Wassenaar Arrangement members in December 2009; this regulatory change eliminates controls under the CCL on "[m]any items in which the use of encryption is ancillary to the primary function of the item"; and
- a provision that makes most encryption technology eligible for export and reexport to non-governmental end-users in countries other than those of "greater national security concern."

According to the June 2010 announcement of the EAR amendment, the United States "will also review other issues related to encryption controls."

The Obama Administration is currently developing new proposals to decontrol additional items. However, such measures would require approval by the members of the Wassenaar Arrangement.

CONGRESSIONAL ACTIVITY

Satellites

During the 2nd session of the 112th Congress, the National Defense Authorization Act (NDAA) of 2013 (P.L. 112-239, January 2, 2013) included a provision to repeal Section 1513(a) of the Strom Thurmond NDAA of 1999, which removed satellites and related items from the Commerce Control List (CCL) and placed them on the U.S. Munitions List (USML). This provision has the effect of allowing the President to determine the jurisdiction of the satellites and related items that were transferred at that time, potentially allowing the President to transfer them back to the CCL subject to certain determinations and reporting requirements. (See text box, "Commercial Communications Satellites," above)

Export Control Reform Legislation

In addition, two bills were introduced to reform the U.S. export control regime in the 112th Congress. One would have reauthorized the Export Administration Act (EAA) and would have amended some of its provisions, as well as amended certain provisions in the Arms Export Control Act (AECA) governing munitions licensing. The other would have replaced the EAA with a new act that would have provided the President the authority to create—within certain guidelines—a new dual-use export control licensing system. Each bill would have implications for the President's export control initiative and may be reintroduced in the 113th Congress in whole or in part. In addition, the Administration may put forward legislation to implement portions of the Export Control Reform Initiative.

Export Administration Renewal Act of 2011

The Export Administration Renewal Act of 2011 (H.R. 2122) was introduced by House Foreign Affairs Committee (HFAC) Chairwoman Ros-Lehtinen on June 03, 2011. The legislation would have renewed the currently expired Export Administration Act through 2015, would have increased the penalty structure consistent with current IEEPA penalties, and would have provided enhanced statutory investigative and overseas enforcement authority to the Department of Commerce, consistent with the Comprehensive Iran Sanctions and Divestment Act of 2010 (P.L. 111-195). The bill also would have amended the EAA's foreign policy controls to extend the period of time to 36 months that a government previously designated as a state sponsor of terrorism must abstain from acts of terrorism before it can be removed from that designation. In addition, it would have provided for congressional oversight by requiring that "significant" proposed regulations be submitted to the committees of jurisdiction (House Foreign Affairs, Senate Banking) for a 30-day period of advanced review.

Title II would have permitted generic parts and components for defense articles on the U.S. Munitions List to be treated differently than sensitive defense articles on the USML if such parts and components "do not have specialized or unique military or intelligence capabilities or significance." Items removed from the USML would have been subject to the same level of control as on the USML unless the President determined that it was (1) in the national interest to do so and (2) complied with notification requirements in the EAA, and (3) a consensus-based interagency process between State, Commerce, and Defense determined the subsequent level of control of items removed from the USML. Items removed from the USML would have also faced heightened restrictions to certain countries. Licenses for items removed from the USML on the Wassennaar Sensitive and Very Sensitive Lists would have faced a presumption of denial to China unless the President issues a national interest waiver and adheres to congressional notification requirements. In addition, a license for any item removed from the USML under this process would have been denied to any country subject to U.N. or U.S. sanctions, or prohibited from purchasing arms from the United States under the ITAR.

Technology Security Act of 2012

On May 26, 2011, HFAC Ranking Member Berman introduced the Technology Security Act of 2011 (H.R. 2004), touted as the "the first comprehensive export control legislation to be proposed since 2001."[53] The legislation would have given the President the authority to control exports for national security and foreign policy reasons generally, including the prevention of proliferation of weapons of mass destruction, the prevention of terrorism, and the prevention of activities designed to interfere or disrupt critical infrastructure. The legislation would have asserted that U.S. national security required the maintenance of leadership and competitiveness in the science, technology, and manufacturing sectors and that the implementation of export controls should be evaluated on an ongoing basis, and that export controls should be implemented on a multilateral basis (§102).

In exercising his authority to export controls, the President would have been directed to establish and maintain lists of items subject to control, lists of foreign persons or end-uses subject to control, licensing criteria and licensing alternatives—such as advanced notice in lieu of licensing, and compliance and enforcement measures. It would have expanded the definition of dual-use items to include those that could be used for cyber or terrorist attacks. The legislation would have established penalties consistent with the IEEPA penalties (see above). The legislation also would have directed the President to establish an inter-agency Transfer Policy Committee to identify strategic threats requiring export controls and to implement policies to counter those threats. This committee also would have been charged with regularly reviewing the control list and establishing and maintaining a licensing system. The legislation would have required the President to maintain current license requirements on countries supporting international terrorism, as well as current sanctions regarding missile proliferation and chemical and biological weapons proliferation. It also would have reauthorized the anti-boycott provisions from the EAA.

The Technology Security Act (H.R. 2004) would have given the President wide discretion in the creation of a dual-use export system. Under this legislation, the President would have been given the authority to establish such a system and to determine where it would be located in the government. Conversely, the President could have maintained the current system with some changes, such as the creation of the Transfer Policy Committee under the new authority. By contrast, the EAA Reauthorization Act (H.R. 2122) would have locked in the current dual-use system and updated some features of it. Passage of this act likely would have prevented the establishment of a unified licensing agency envisioned by the Administration as the EAA vests the dual-use system with the Secretary of Commerce. It also may have affected efforts to streamline enforcement, as the EAA confers certain powers to the Commerce Department to enforce export controls. However, neither act would amend or modify the organizational aspects of the munitions licensing process.

In considering any new legislation and the President's proposals, Congress could consider how to balance between national security and economic competitiveness in a changing global environment. In addition, Congress could address the benefits and costs of continuing the current bifurcated export control system or the creation of a unified system. At the same time, it may wish to scrutinize the current system administered under emergency authority. It may examine the relationship between U.S. multilateral non-proliferation commitments and the current export control regime. Congress may assess the ability to maintain the U.S. defense industrial base in terms of the current system, as well as the competitiveness of U.S. strategic sectors. These strategic, institutional, and economic considerations may shape the future of U.S. export controls.

APPENDIX A. BASIC EXPORT CONTROL CHARACTERISTICS

Characteristic	Dual-Use	Munitions	Nuclear
Legislative Authority	Export Administration Act (EAA) of 1979 (expired); International Emergency Economic Powers Act of 1977 (IEEPA)	Arms Export Control Act of 1968, 1976 (AECA)	Atomic Energy Act of 1954; Nuclear Non-Proliferation Act of 1978
Agency of Jurisdiction	Bureau of Industry and Security (BIS)(Commerce)	Directorate of Defense Trade Controls (DDTC)(State)	Nuclear Regulatory Commission (NRC) (facilities and material) Department of Energy (DOE) (technology) BIS ("outside the core" civilian power plant equipment) DDTC (nuclear items in defense articles)
Implementing Regulations	Export Administration Regulations (EAR) (15 C.F.R. 730 et seq)	International Traffic in Arms Regulations (ITAR) (22 C.F.R. 120 et seq)	10 C.F.R. 110—Export and Import of Nuclear Material and Equipment (NRC) 10 C.F.R. 810—Assistance to Foreign Atomic Energy Activities (DOE)
Control List	Commerce Control List (CCL)	Munitions List (USML)	List of Nuclear Facilities and Equipment; List of Nuclear Materials (NRC) Nuclear Referral List (CCL) USML Activities Requiring Specific Authorization (DOE)

Appendix A. (Continued)

Characteristic	Dual-Use	Munitions	Nuclear
Relation to Multilateral Controls	Wassenaar Arrangement (dual-use) Missile Technology Control Regime (MTCR) Australia Group (CBW) Nuclear Suppliers' Group	Wassenaar Arrangement (munitions) MTCR	Nuclear Suppliers' Group International Atomic Energy Agency
Licensing Policy	Based on item, country, or both. Anti-terrorism controls proscribe exports to five countries for nearly all CCL listings	Most Munitions License items require licenses; 21 proscribed countries.	General/Specific Licenses (NRC) General/Specific Authorizations (DOE)
Licensing Application Timeline	Initial referral within nine days; agency must approve/deny within 30 days; 90-day appeal process (see Appendix B)	60 days with national security exceptions; congressional notification period for significant military equipment	No timeframe for license applications
Enforcement	Office of Export Enforcement (BIS) (OEE) (domestic) Homeland Security (DHS): Immigration and Customs Enforcement (ICE); Customs and Border Protection (CBP) Justice (DOJ): National Security Division; FBI	Office of Defense Trade Compliance (DDTC) Defense Criminal Investigation Service (DCIS)(DOD) Defense Security Service (DOD) DHS: ICE, CBP DOJ: National Security Division; FBI	Office of Enforcement (NRC) BIS-OEE DDTC-ODTC DCIS (DOD) DHS: ICE, CBP DOJ: National Security Division; FBI
Penalties	Criminal: $1 million/20 years imprisonment Civil: $250,000/Denial of export privileges (IEEPA)	Criminal: $1 million/10 years imprisonment Civil: $500,000/forfeiture of goods, conveyance Denial of export privileges for either	Criminal: Individual—$250,000/12 years to life imprisonment; Firm—$500,000 (NRC and DOE) Civil: $100,000 per violation (NRC)

Source: Congressional Research Service (CRS).

Appendix B. Dual-Use Export Licensing Process

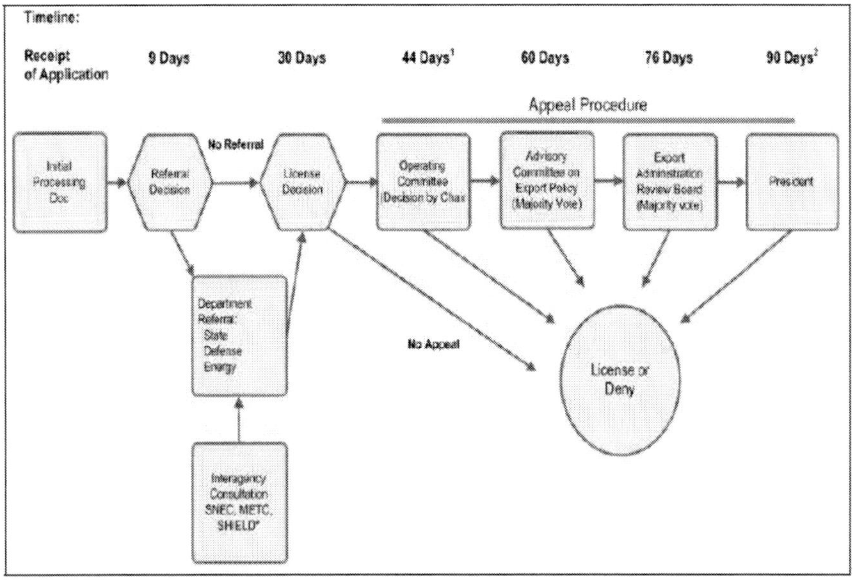

Source: Prepared by Ian F. Fergusson, Congressional Research Service (CRS).

Notes:

[1]The time periods for the appeal procedure reflect a five-day window of appeal and an 11-day period for each body to make a decision.

[2]A license application must be resolved or appealed to the President within 90 days. The order does place a time limit on a presidential decision.

*SNEC, Sub-Groups on Nuclear Export Policy, MTEC, Missile Technology/Export Control Group; SHIELD Chemical and Biological Weapons Control Group.

Figure B-1. Dual-Use Export Licensing Process; (Executive Order 12981, December 1995).

Appendix C. List of Acronyms

AECA—Arms Export Control Act
AES—Automated Export System
BIS—Bureau of Industry and Security, Department of Commerce
CBP—Customs and Border Protection, Department of Homeland Security
CCL—Commerce Control List
CML—Commerce Munitions List

CPI—Counter-Proliferation Investigations
CW—Chemical Weapons
DCIS—Defense Criminal Investigation Service
DDTC—Directorate of Defense Trade Controls, Department of State
DHS—Department of Homeland Security
DOJ—Department of Justice
DTSA—Defense Technology Security Administration
EAA—Export Administration Act
EAR—Export Administration Regulations
ECCN—Export Control Classification Number
EECC—Export Enforcement Coordination Center
EEB—Economic, Energy, and Business Bureau, Department of State
FP—Foreign Policy Controls
GAO—Governmental Accountability Office
IEEPA—International Emergency Economic Powers Act
ICE—Immigration and Customs Enforcement Agency, Department of Homeland Security
ISN—International Security and Nonproliferation Bureau, Department of State
ITA—International Trade Administration, Department of Commerce
ITAR—International Traffic in Arms Regulations
MTCR—Missile Technology Control Regime
NEECN—National Export Enforcement Coordination Network
NRC—Nuclear Regulatory Commission
NS—National Security Controls
NSG—Nuclear Suppliers Group
OEE—Office of Export Enforcement
ODTC—Office of Defense Trade Compliance, DDTC
OFAC—Office of Foreign Assets Control, Department of the Treasury
SI—Significant Items Controls
SL—Surreptitious Listening Controls
SS—Short Supply Controls
STA—Strategic Trade Authorization
USML—U.S. Munitions List

APPENDIX D. PROPOSED MIGRATION OF CERTAIN USML ITEMS TO THE CCL

Table D-1. Proposed Migration Table

USML Category	Proposed CCL Destination	Status: Date/Federal Register
Category IV: launch vehicles, missiles, rockets, torpedoes, bombs, mines, and other military explosive devices	Category 0: Nuclear Materials, Facilities and Equipment, and Miscellaneous; Category 9: Aerospace and Propulsion	Proposed January 16, 2013: 78 Fed. Reg. 6750 (EAR), 78 Fed. Reg. 6765 (ITAR)
Category V: Explosives and Energetic Materials, Propellants, Incendiary Agents and Their Constituents	Category 1: Materials, Chemicals, "Microorganisms", Toxins	Proposed May 2, 2012: 77 Fed. Reg. 25932 (EAR), 77 Fed. Reg. 25944.
Category VI: Vessels of War and Naval Equipment	Category 8: Marine; Category 9 (GTE)	Proposed December 23, 2011: 76 Fed. Reg. 80291(EAR); 76 Fed. Reg. 80302 (ITAR)
Category VII: Tanks and Military Vehicles	Category 0: Nuclear Materials, Facilities and Equipment, and Miscellaneous; Category 9 (GTE)	Proposed July 15, 2011: 76 Fed. Reg. 41957 (EAR); Revision: December 6, 2011: 76 Fed. Reg. 76085 (ITAR); 76 Fed. Reg. 76085 (EAR)
Category VIII: Aircraft and Associated Equipment	Category 9: Propulsion Systems, Space Vehicles, and Related Items	Proposed November 7, 2011: 76 Fed. Reg. 68675 (EAR); 76 Fed. Reg. 68694 (ITAR); Final Rule, April 16, 2013: 78 Fed. Reg. 22660 (EAR), 78 Fed. Reg. 22740 (ITAR).
Category IX: Military Training Equipment	Category 0: Nuclear Materials, Facilities and Equipment, and Miscellaneous;	Proposed June 13, 2012: 77 Fed. Reg. 35310 (EAR); 77 Fed. Reg. 35319 (ITAR)
Category X: Protective Personal Equipment and Shelters	Category 1: Materials, Chemicals, "Microorganisms", Toxins	Proposed June 7, 2012: 77 Fed. Reg. 33688 (EAR); 77 Fed. Reg. 33698 (ITAR)
Category XI: Military Electronics (Includes certain cryogenic and superconductive eq. operated in motion in Cats. VI,VII,VIII & XV)	Category 3: Electronics; Category 9: Aerospace and Propulsion	Proposed November 28, 2012: 77 Fed. Reg. 70945 (EAR); 77 Fed. Reg. 70958(ITAR)
Category XIII: Auxiliary Military Equipment	Category 0: Nuclear Materials, Facilities and Equipment, and Miscellaneous;	Proposed May 18, 2012: 77 Fed. Reg. 28250 (EAR); 77 Fed. Reg. 29575 (ITAR);

Table D-1. (Continued)

USML Category	Proposed CCL Destination	Status: Date/Federal Register
Category XVI: Nuclear Weapons Related articles.	Category 1: nuclear materials; some items also under NRC, Energy Dept. control.	Proposed January 30, 2013: 78 Fed. Reg. 6269 (ITAR)
Category XIX: Gas Turbine Engines (GTE) (New category consolidating GTE from Categories VI, VII, VIII).	Category 9: Aerospace and Propulsion	Proposed December 6, 2011: 76 Fed. Reg. 76072 (EAR); 76 Fed. Reg. 76097 (ITAR); Final Rule, April 16, 2013: 78 Fed. Reg. 22660 (EAR); 78 Fed. Reg. 22740 (ITAR).
Category XX: Submersible Vessels and Oceanic Equipment	Category 8: Marine	Proposed December 23, 2011: 76 Fed. Reg. 80291 (EAR); 76 Fed. Reg. 80305 (ITAR)

Source: Congressional Research Service.
Note: GTE: Gas Turbine Engine.

End Notes

[1] International Traffic in Arms Regulations, 22 C.F.R. 120.3.

[2] U.S. Government Accountability Office (GAO), High-Risk Series: An Update, GAO-07-310, January 2010. While GAO noted some improvements, the export control system was still considered a "high-risk" area in 2011; see GAO, High-Risk Series: An Update, GAO-11-278, February 2011.

[3] "Ros-Lehtinen Skeptical of Scope, Pace of Export Control Reform Initiative," Inside U.S. Trade, May 13, 2011.

[4] Webcast available at http://foreignaffairs.house.gov/hearing_notice.asp?id=1399.

[5] "Background and Key Provisions of the Technology Security Act," http://democrats.foreignaffairs.house.gov/ press_display.asp?id=844.

[6] This national emergency was most recently continued until August 17, 2013, by President Obama on August 15, 2012, 77 Federal Register 49699, August 16, 2012.

[7] Under IEEPA authority, the President may "investigate, block during the pendency of an investigation, regulate, direct and compel, nullify, void, prevent or prohibit, any acquisition, holding, withholding, use, transfer, withdrawal, transportation, importation or exportation of, or dealing in, or exercising any right, power, or privilege with respect to, or transactions involving, any property in which any foreign country or a national thereof has any interest by any person, or with respect to any property, subject to the jurisdiction of the United States." P.L. 95-223, §203(a)(1)(B).

[8] This authority was previously vested with Secretary of State.

[9] U.S. Government Accountability Office (GAO), High-Risk Series: An Update, GAO-11-278, February 2011.

[10] For more information about these regimes, see CRS Report RL33865, Arms Control and Nonproliferation: A Catalog of Treaties and Agreements, by Amy F. Woolf, Mary Beth Nikitin, and Paul K. Kerr.

[11] "Commerce Control List: Revising Descriptions of Items and Foreign Availability," 75 Federal Register, No. 236, December 9, 2010.

[12] The Nonproliferation Treaty (NPT) defines a nuclear-weapon state as "one which has manufactured and exploded a nuclear weapon or other nuclear explosive device" prior to January 1, 1967. These states are China, France, Russia, the United Kingdom, and the United States.

[13] Remarks of BIS Assistant Secretary for Export Administration, Kevin Wolf, to Exportkontrolltag 2011, Munich, Germany, February 25, 2011.

[14] Secretary of Defense Robert M. Gates, speech before the Business Executives for National Security, April 20, 2010, available at http://www.defense.gov/speeches/speech.aspx?speechid=1453.

[15] Discussion with National Security Council official, March 18, 2011.

[16] For example, determining the appropriateness of releasing technical data to employees of a foreign firm engaged in a defense project with a U.S. firm.

[17] Government Accountability Office, Export Controls: Observations on Selected Countries' Systems and Proposed Treaties, May 2010, GAO-10-557.

[18] The State Department's Directorate of Defense Trade Controls, according to the GAO, "considers a third-country national to be an individual from a country other than the country which is the foreign signatory" to a "technical assistance or manufacturing license agreement. A third-country national may also be a dual national if he or she holds nationality from more than one country." GAO-10-557.

[19] "Amendment to the International Traffic in Arms Regulations: Dual Nationals and Third-Country Nationals Employed by End-Users," Federal Register, vol. 75, no. 154, August 11, 2010, p. 48625.

[20] Ibid.

[21] "International Traffic in Arms Regulations: Dual Nationals and Third-Country Nationals Employed by End-Users," Federal Register, vol. 76, no. 94, May 16, 2011, p.28174. Paul Conlin, Sebastien Beauregard, R. Luc Beaulieu, and Richard A. Wagner, "Proposed ITAR Amendment Regarding Dual Nationals and Third-Country Nationals," Mondaq, August 31, 2010.

[22] "Substantive contacts," according to the rule, "include regular travel to such countries, recent or continuing contact with agents, brokers, and nationals of such countries, continued demonstrated allegiance to such countries, maintenance of business relationships with persons from such countries, maintenance of a residence in such countries, receiving salary or other continuing monetary compensation from such countries, or acts otherwise indicating a risk of diversion."

[23] Federal Register, vol. 75, no. 154.

[24] "Revisions to the U.S. Munitions List, Advanced Notice of Proposed Rulemaking," 75 Federal Register 76935, December 9, 2010, at 76937.

[25] As originally postulated, Tier 1 articles are those that are almost exclusively available from the United States and provide a critical military or intelligence advantage. Tier 2 articles are those that are almost exclusively available from countries that are members of the multilateral export control regimes that control such items and (1) provide a substantial military or intelligence advantage, or (2) make a substantial contribution to the indigenous development, production, use, or enhancement of a Tier 1 or Tier 2 item. Tier 3 articles are those that provide a significant military or intelligence advantage; make a significant contribution to the indigenous development, production, use, or enhancement of a Tier 1,

Tier 2, or Tier 3 item; or are otherwise controlled for national security, foreign policy, or human rights reasons.

[26] "Administration Identifies Problem, Alters Stance on Export Control Reform," Inside U.S. Trade, November 3, 2011.

[27] "Revisions to the Export Administration Regulations (EAR): Initial Implementation of Export Control Reform," 78 Fed. Reg. 22660, April 16, 2013. This rulemaking, which will come into effect on October 16, 2013, also incorporates the final "framework rule" on the "600 series," the "specially designed rule" and other changes to the EAR.

[28] "Revisions to the Export Administration Regulations: ECCN 0Y521 Series," 77 Federal Register 22191, April 13, 2012.

[29] Remarks of BIS Assistant Secretary for Export Administration Kevin Wolf to the Update 2011Conference; Washington D.C.; July 19, 2011.

[30] "Proposed Revisions to the Export Administration Regulations: Control of Items the President Determines No Longer Warrant Control Under the U.S. Munitions List," Proposed Rule, 76 Federal Register 41958, July 15, 2011.

[31] The 600 Series has also been referred to as the Commerce Munitions List. Series 600 items are to be designated with a 6 in the ECCN. For example, applicable aircraft will have a 9A610 ECCN.

[32] Export Administration Regulations, Part 772.2(b).

[33] "Revisions to the Export Administration Regulations: Initial Implementation of Export Control Reform," 78 Fed. Reg. 22660, April 16, 2013; "Revisions to the International Traffic in Arms Regulations: Initial Implementation of Export Control Reforms," 78 Fed. Reg. 22740, April 16, 2013.

[34] Ibid.

[35] Ibid.

[36] Remarks of Kevin Wolf, Assistant Secretary for Export Administration, to the Update 2012 Conference, July 17, 2012. http://www.bis.doc.gov/news/2012/wolf_update_2012.htm.

[37] "Feasibility of Enumerating "Specially Designed" Components," 77 Federal Register 36419, June 19, 2012.

[38] "Export Control Reform Initiative: Strategic Trade Authorization License Exception," 76 Federal Register 35276, June 16, 2011.

[39] However, the final rule excludes NS controlled items from the Wassenaar Arrangement's Sensitive List to the 8 countries.

[40] BIS Press Release, June 16, 2011, http://www.bis.doc.gov/news/2011/bis_press06162011.htm.

[41] Speech of General Jim Jones, June 30, 2010, available at http://www.aia-aerospace speech_jones_06302010.pdf.

[42] Department of Commerce, Press Release, March 7, 2012. http://export.gov/static/2012-03-07%20Commerce%20on%20ITU_Latest_eg_main_047470.pdf.

[43] Department of Justice Press, Release, June 20, 2007, http://www.justice.gov/opa /pr/2007/June/07_nsd_440.html.

[44] Conversation with NSC Official, March 18, 2011.

[45] "DOD Official Says Single IT System for Export Controls Still Being Tested," Inside U.S. Trade, December 13, 2012.

[46] Export Practitioner, September 2010, p. 22.

[47] "It May Take Two Years to Adopt Single Electronic Licensing System, BISer Says," Export Practitioner, August 2010, p. 26.

[48] "Single Export Application for All Agencies to be Unveiled, White House Official Says," Export Practitioner, January 2011, p. 31.

[49] According to an Administration official, controlling the export of products with encryption capabilities differs from controlling other exports because the United States generally wants to obtain information on exported encryption technology rather than prevent its export.

[50] "Encryption Export Controls: Revision of License Exception ENC and Mass Market Eligibility, Submission Procedures, Reporting Requirements, License Application Requirements, and Addition of Note 4 to Category 5, Part 2," 75 Federal Register 36481, June 25, 2010.

[51] Quotations describing the June 25 announcement are taken from 75 Federal Register, no. 122 and from BIS statements available at http://www.bis.doc.gov/encryption.

[52] The Commerce Department classifies certain products with encryption capabilities as "mass market" pursuant to a procedure described in the EAR.

[53] "Congressman Howard Berman Introduces Overhaul of US Exports Controls," http://democrats.

INDEX

D

P

Q

R

S

T

U

V

W